LAIDLAW
SPELLING

Nancy L. Roser
Professor, Department of Curriculum and Instruction
University of Texas, Austin

LAIDLAW BROTHERS · PUBLISHERS
A Division of Doubleday & Company, Inc.
RIVER FOREST, ILLINOIS
Sacramento, California   Chamblee, Georgia   Dallas, Texas   Toronto, Canada

D1511138

ACKNOWLEDGMENTS

Editorial development, design, production and photo research by
McClanahan & Company in cooperation with Laidlaw Brothers, Publishers

LAIDLAW EDITORIAL STAFF

Editorial Manager W. Harold Walker **Senior Editor** Louisa Jo Olson
Editor Barbara J. Kirby **Manager of Production** Kathleen Kasper
Manager of Art and Design Gloria J. Muczynski

EDUCATOR-REVIEWERS

Vera Ginn
Teacher
Seminole Middle School
Fort Lauderdale, Florida

Robert A. Lee
Curriculum Coordinator for Language Arts
and Reading
Wheaton-Warrenville Community School
District 200
Wheaton, Illinois

Lola LeCounte
Assistant Director of English/Language Arts
Instructional Services Center
Langdon School
Washington, D.C.

Mary Lou Meerson
Principal
Avocado Elementary School
La Mesa, California

Edna Minaya
Coordinator of Language Arts
Metropolitan School District
Nashville, Tennessee

Reverend John F. Murphy
Superintendent of Education
Diocese of Cleveland
Cleveland, Ohio

Cathy Rutledge
Teacher
East Elementary School
Jefferson City, Missouri

Carmen H. Salazar
Coordinator of Curriculum Development
Dallas Independent School District
Dallas, Texas

Marilyn Stuart
Director of the Middle School
Calhoun School
New York, New York

The pronunciation key used in the Speller Dictionary is from *Scott, Foresman Beginning Dictionary*,
E.L. Thorndike and Clarence L. Barnhart. Copyright © 1983 by Scott, Foresman and Company.
Reprinted by permission.

Handwriting models in this book are reproduced with permission of Zaner-Bloser, Inc., from the series
HANDWRITING: Basic Skills and Application, © 1984.

ISBN 0-8445-0502-1

123456789 10 11 12 13 14 15   PRINTED IN THE UNITED STATES OF AMERICA   5432109876

CONTENTS

Adam likes the animal poster. But he isn't sure what it means. One letter mixed up the meaning. The poster should say TO instead of TWO.

Bad spelling causes mix-ups. Good spelling helps you write clearly. It makes your work easier to read.

This book will help you learn to spell. Use it TO get a head start in good spelling.

LEARNING TO SPELL A WORD

1. Look at the word.

2. Say the word.

3. Copy the word.

4. Spell the word aloud.

5. Write the word.

1. _____

2. _____

3. _____

4. _____

5. _____

6. _____

7. _____

8. _____

9. _____

10. _____

1. lap

2. map

3. man

4. mad

5. bad

6. hat

7. pat

8. ram

9. jam

10. gas

1 MAN IN A HAT

FOCUS

Say *man* and *hat*.

Listen for the middle sound.

The middle sound in these words is called the short *a* sound.

The dictionary sign for short *a* is /a/.

Write *man* and *hat*.

1. _____   2. _____

Ring the letter that spells the short *a* sound in each word.

CHALLENGE

as   dash

has   cash

path

2

LEARN

Name the picture.

Write two core words that rhyme with each picture name.

bat

1. _____ 2. _____

clam

3. _____ 4. _____

cap

5. _____ 6. _____

glad

7. _____ 8. _____

Write one core word that rhymes with each picture name.

pan

9. _____

glass

10. _____

CHALLENGE WORDS

Write two rhyming pairs of challenge words.

1. _____ 2. _____

3. _____ 4. _____

Write the challenge word that rhymes with *bath*.

5. _____

3

PRACTICE   Write the core word that goes with the clue.

1. use this on a trip

   _____

   _ _ _ _ _ _ _ _

   _____

2. head cover

   _____

   _ _ _ _ _ _ _ _

   _____

3. angry

   _____

   _ _ _ _ _ _ _ _

   _____

4. makes a car go

   _____

   _ _ _ _ _ _ _ _

   _____

5. put this on bread

   _____

   _ _ _ _ _ _ _ _

   _____

6. male sheep

   _____

   _ _ _ _ _ _ _ _

   _____

7. tap with your hand

   _____

   _ _ _ _ _ _ _ _

   _____

8. a dad

   _____

   _ _ _ _ _ _ _ _

   _____

9. not good

   _____

   _ _ _ _ _ _ _ _

   _____

10. you have this when you sit

   _____

   _ _ _ _ _ _ _ _

   _____

WRITE WORD FAMILIES

Add the letters *at* to make words.

1. c ___

2. b ___

3. m ___

Add the letters *an* to make words.

4. f ___

5. c ___

6. r ___

4

COMMUNICATE

PROOFREAD

Each sentence has one spelling mistake.
Find each mistake.
Write the word right.

This mann is Larry. He looks med, doesn't he? Well, he's had a badd day. First, he lost his mape. Next, he ran out of ges. Now he's in a traffic gam!

WRITE RIGHT

All your letters should sit on the bottom line.
Write this sentence.

Larry is mad.

_____

- - - - - - - - - - -

_____

1. _____
2. _____
3. _____
4. _____
5. _____
6. _____

WRITE ON YOUR OWN

Have you had a day when many things went wrong? Tell about your bad day. Spell the words as well as you can. Make sure all your letters sit on the bottom line.

5

1. _____

2. _____

3. _____

4. _____

5. _____

6. _____

7. _____

8. _____

9. _____

10. _____

1. if

2. fix

3. mix

4. pin

5. rip

6. tip

7. zip

8. his

9. kiss

10. milk

CHALLENGE

dish	mitt
fish	rich
wish	

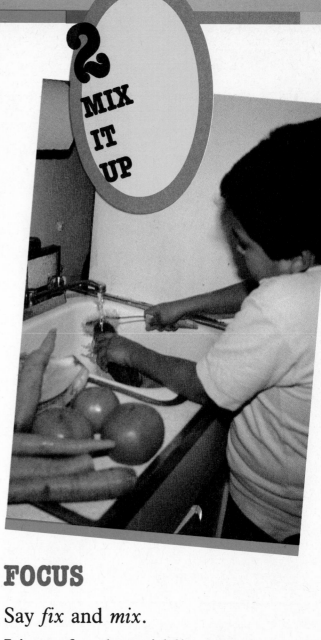

2 MIX IT UP

FOCUS

Say *fix* and *mix*.
Listen for the middle sound.
The middle sound in these
words is called the short *i* sound.
The sign for short *i* is /i/.
Write *fix* and *mix*.

_____ _____

1. _____ 2. _____

Ring the letter that spells the
short *i* sound in each word.

6

LEARN

What letter belongs in the blue box?
Think of the letter. Write the core
words.

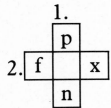

1.
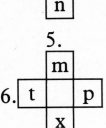

2. f ___ x
(p / n)

1. _____

_____

2. _____

3.
z
4. ___ f
p

3. _____

4. _____

5.
m
6. t ___ p
x

5. _____

_____

6. _____

8. k
r ___ p
s
s

7. _____

_____

8. _____

9.
h
10. m ___ l k
s

9. _____

_____

10. _____

CHALLENGE WORDS

Write three challenge words that
rhyme.

1. _____   2. _____   3. _____

Write the challenge word that rhymes
with each word.

which   4. _____   sit   5. _____

PRACTICE   Write the missing core words.

1. _____ a bike

2. _____ a zipper

3. _____ a hole

4. _____ a cow

5. _____ red and blue

6. _____ the baby

7. _____ over the glass

8. _____ the tail on the donkey

Come to __(9)__ party __(10)__ you can.

WRITE WORD FAMILIES

Add the letters *in* to make words.

1. f _____

2. w _____

3. b _____

Add the letters *ip* to make words.

4. l _____

5. s _____

PROOFREAD

Find two spelling mistakes.
Write the words right.

French Toast

1 egg   3 tablespoons milk

2 slices bread   1 tablespoon butter

First, mixx egg and melk. dip in
bread. Melt butter in pan. Fry bread
on both sides.

1. _____

2. _____

Begin a sentence with a capital letter.
One sentence in the recipe does not begin
with a capital letter. Write it correctly.

_____

_____

_____

CORE WORDS

if
fix
mix
pin
rip
tip
zip
his
kiss
milk

WRITE RIGHT

Dot your *i*'s
correctly.

mix   mix   mix

not clear   not clear   clear

Write this sentence.   Mix in the milk.

_____

_____

WRITE ON YOUR OWN

Tell about a time you helped make a
meal. Begin each sentence with a
capital letter.

9

1. _____
2. _____
3. _____
4. _____
5. _____
6. _____
7. _____
8. _____
9. _____
10. _____

1. cot
2. got
3. lot
4. spot
5. dog
6. fog
7. log
8. jog
9. job
10. flop

robin   cross
soggy   off
slot

10

3 JOG WITH A DOG

FOCUS

Say *lot*.

Listen for the middle sound.
The middle sound in this word
is called the short *o* sound. The
sign for short *o* is /o/.

Write *lot*.   _____

Ring the letter   1. _____

that spells the short *o* sound.

Say *dog*.

Listen for the middle sound.
The sign for the middle sound
in this word is /ô/.

Write *dog*.   _____

Ring the letter   2. _____

that spells the vowel sound in
dog. The vowel sounds for *lot*
and *dog* are both spelled with
the letter *o*.

LEARN

Write four core words that rhyme
with *pot*.

_____   _____   _____   _____

‒ ‒ ‒ ‒ ‒ ‒ ‒ ‒   ‒ ‒ ‒ ‒ ‒ ‒ ‒ ‒   ‒ ‒ ‒ ‒ ‒ ‒ ‒ ‒   ‒ ‒ ‒ ‒ ‒ ‒ ‒ ‒
1. _____   2. _____   3. _____   4. _____

Write four core words with the same
ending sound as the picture name.

_____   _____   _____   _____

‒ ‒ ‒ ‒ ‒ ‒ ‒ ‒   ‒ ‒ ‒ ‒ ‒ ‒ ‒ ‒   ‒ ‒ ‒ ‒ ‒ ‒ ‒ ‒   ‒ ‒ ‒ ‒ ‒ ‒ ‒ ‒
5. _____   6. _____   7. _____   8. _____

Write one core word with the same
ending sound as each picture name.

_____   _____

‒ ‒ ‒ ‒ ‒ ‒ ‒ ‒   ‒ ‒ ‒ ‒ ‒ ‒ ‒ ‒
9. _____   10. _____

CHALLENGE WORDS

Write the challenge word that goes
with the clue.

_____   _____

‒ ‒ ‒ ‒ ‒ ‒ ‒ ‒   ‒ ‒ ‒ ‒ ‒ ‒ ‒ ‒
1. bird   _____   2. go to other side   _____

_____   _____

‒ ‒ ‒ ‒ ‒ ‒ ‒ ‒   ‒ ‒ ‒ ‒ ‒ ‒ ‒ ‒
3. not on   _____   4. small opening   _____

_____

‒ ‒ ‒ ‒ ‒ ‒ ‒ ‒
5. wet   _____

Ring the letter that spells short *o*
or /ô/ in each word.

PRACTICE

Read the story.

Write the missing core words.

After you work hard at a ___(1)___, you
may be tired. But don't ___(2)___ down
on a chair! Don't lie down on a ___(3)___.
Go outside and ___(4)___. Take a run
with your ___(5)___. You will feel a ___(6)___
better! You will be glad that you
___(7)___ out.

Answer each question with a core
word.

8. What burns in the fireplace?
9. What makes it hard to see
    outdoors?
10. What do you get on your shirt if
    you spill your juice?

1. _____ 2. _____

3. _____ 4. _____

5. _____ 6. _____

7. _____ 8. _____

9. _____ 10. _____

WRITE WORD FAMILIES

Add the letters *op* to make words.

 1. t_____   2. m_____   3. st_____

Add the letters *ot* to make words.

Do 4. n_____ go near the 5. p_____. It is 6. h_____.

12

COMMUNICATE

DICTIONARY WORKOUT

Words in a dictionary are in ABC order:

a b c d e f g h i j k l m n o p q r s t u v w x y z

Write the letter that comes before.

1. 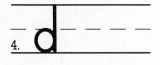 c

2. 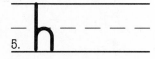 |

3.  t

Write the letter that comes after.

4. d

5. h

6. v

Write the letters in ABC order.

f h e g   7. _____

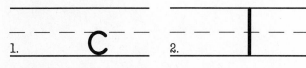

WRITE RIGHT

All your tall letters should touch the top line.
Write the six core words with tall letters.

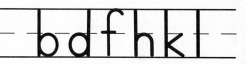

b d f h k l

1. _____

2. _____

3. _____

4. _____

5. _____

6. _____

WRITE ON YOUR OWN

What sport do you like best? Tell about that sport. Spell the words as well as you can. Make sure your tall letters touch the top line.

CORE WORDS

cot
got
lot
spot
dog
fog
log
jog
job
flop

13

1. _____	1. dock
2. _____	2. rock
3. _____	3. lock
4. _____	4. pack
5. _____	5. sack
6. _____	6. kick
7. _____	7. sick
8. _____	8. stick
9. _____	9. stack
10. _____	10. snack

CHALLENGE

click   shack

clock   backpack

flock

4 PACK A SNACK

FOCUS

Say *pack* and *snack*.
Listen for the ending sound.
Write *pack* and *snack*.

1. _____

2. _____

Ring the letters that spell
the ending sound in each word.

LEARN

Which letter makes a word?
Write the core words.
Ring the *ck* endings.

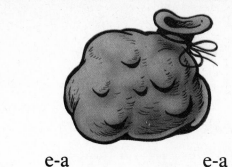

a-o
1. d | | c | k
_____
- - - - - -

i-e
2. s | | c | k
_____
- - - - - -

e-a
3. s | t | | c | k
_____
- - - - - -

e-a
4. s | | c | k
_____
- - - - - -

i-e
5. s | t | | c | k
_____
- - - - - -

u-o
6. r | | c | k
_____
- - - - - -

a-o
7. p | | c | k
_____
- - - - - -

e-o
8. l | | c | k
_____
- - - - - -

a-i
9. k | | c | k
_____
- - - - - -

a-e
10. s | n | | c | k
_____
- - - - - -

CHALLENGE WORDS

Write the challenge words that rhyme
with the picture names.
Ring the *ck* endings.

(2 words)   1. _____   2. _____

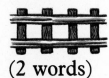

(2 words)   3. _____   4. _____   (1 word)   5. _____

15

PRACTICE

Write the missing core words.

Take a good ___(1)___ to school. You can ___(2)___ it in a backpack. You can put it in a ___(3)___ or bag. Take a carrot ___(4)___ or an apple. Then you will be ready to ___(5)___ a ball.

Write the core word that goes with each clue.

1. opens with a key

_____

2. not well

_____

3. a stone

_____

4. a high pile

_____

5. a place to park a boat

_____

1. _____

2. _____

3. _____

4. _____

5. _____

WRITE WORD FAMILIES

Add the letters *ack* to make words.

1.

b_____

2. not front

b_____

3.

t_____

Add the letters *ick* to make words.

4. ____ tock

t_____

5.

w_____

6. choose

p_____

16

DICTIONARY WORKOUT

Words in a dictionary are in ABC order.

Look at the first letter of each word.

Write each set of words in ABC order.

a b c d e f g h i j k l m n o p q r s t u v w x y z

1. snack _____
   dock _____
   pack _____
   _____
   _____
   _____

2. sick _____
   kick _____
   rock _____
   _____
   _____
   _____

dock
rock
lock
pack
sack
kick
sick
stick
stack
snack

WRITE RIGHT

Your short letters should touch the middle line.

aceimnorsuvwxz

Write this sentence. My snack is good for me.

_____

WRITE ON YOUR OWN

What snacks are good for you? Tell about a good snack you like. Spell the words as well as you can.

17

1. _____
2. _____
3. _____
4. _____
5. _____
6. _____
7. _____
8. _____
9. _____
10. _____

1. pond
2. and
3. band
4. hand
5. sand
6. list
7. lost
8. last
9. fast
10. just

5 JUST SAND

FOCUS

Say *sand* and *just*.
Listen for the two ending sounds in each word.
Write *sand* and *just*.

1. _____
2. _____

Ring the letters that spell the two ending sounds in each word.

cast   stand
past   wind
land

18

LEARN

Name the picture.
Write the core word that has the same
beginning sound as each picture name.

1. _____

2. ![axe] _____

3. ![hammer] _____

4. ![saw] _____

5. ![ball] _____

Name the picture.
Write five core words that have the same
ending sounds as the picture name.

6. _____   7. _____   8. _____

9. _____   10. _____

CHALLENGE WORDS

Write the missing challenge words.
Ring the letters that spell the ending
sounds.

I like to __(1)__ by the lake. I __(2)__
my line into the water. It reaches out
__(3)__ the dock. I hear the __(4)__ in the
trees. Will I bring a fish to __(5)__ ?

1. _____

2. _____

3. _____

4. _____

5. _____

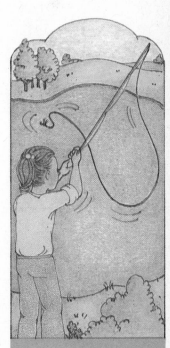

PRACTICE Finish each phrase with a core word.

1. ＿＿ and found

2. salt ＿＿ pepper

3. a ＿＿ castle

4. first and ＿＿

5. a shopping ＿＿

6. ＿＿ as a deer

7. 5 fingers on a ＿＿

8. play drums in the ＿＿

9. swim in the ＿＿

10. She ＿＿ left.

WRITE WORD FAMILIES Make the words mean more than one.
Add the letter *s*.

1. band ＿＿＿＿＿＿

2. hand ＿＿＿＿＿＿

3. list ＿＿＿＿＿＿

4. pond ＿＿＿＿＿＿

5. snack ＿＿＿＿＿＿

6. rock ＿＿＿＿＿＿

COMMUNICATE

DICTIONARY WORKOUT

Words in a dictionary are in ABC order.

Look at the first letter of each word.

Write each set of words in ABC order.

a b c d e f g h i j k l m n o p q r s t u v w x y z

1. band _____
   fast _____
   and _____
   _____
   _____
   _____

2. sand _____
   lost _____
   hand _____
   _____
   _____
   _____

WRITE RIGHT

Write tails on letters clearly.
Write each letter two times.

g j p q y

g   j   p   q   y

WRITE ON YOUR OWN

Tell about a day you spent playing with sand or water. Were you at a park, a beach, or a sandbox?
Spell the words as well as you can.

21

Remember the short *a* sound as in *cat*.
Write the three rhyming pairs of words.

hat
ram
mad
bad
jam
pat

1. _____   2. _____

3. _____   4. _____

5. _____   6. _____

FOCUS

Ring the letter that spells the short *a*
sound in each word.

Remember the short *i* sound as in *six*.
Write the six words that rhyme with these words.

fix
tip
kiss
milk
pin
if

1. miss _____   2. zip _____

3. mix _____   4. sniff _____

5. win _____   6. silk _____

FOCUS   Ring the letter that spells the short *i*
sound in each word.

UNIT 3

Remember the /o/ as in *hop* and the /ô/ as in *hog*.

Write the rhyming groups of words.

cot
dog
got
lot
log
fog

1. _____   2. _____   3. _____

4. _____   5. _____   6. _____

FOCUS Ring the letter that spells the vowel sound in each word.

UNIT 4

Remember the ending sound in *back*.
Write the word pairs with the same beginning sounds as each picture name.

kick
stack
sack
dock
sick
stick

 1. _____   2. _____

  3. _____   4. _____

Write the word that has the same beginning sound as each picture name.

  5. _____   6. _____

FOCUS Ring the two letters that spell the ending sound in each word.

23

Remember the ending sounds of *st* in
last and of *nd* in *land*.
Write the three words that rhyme.

last

hand

band
_____ _____ _____
1._____ 2._____ 3._____

list

lost
Write the three words with the same
beginning sound.

sand
_____ _____ _____
4._____ 5._____ 6._____

FOCUS

Ring the two letters that spell the
ending sounds in each word.

WRITE WORD FAMILIES

Drop the first letter of each word.
Write the new words.

1. hat _____c_____   2. rat _____f_____

3. fix _____s_____   4. got _____h_____

5. sick _____p_____   6. hand _____l_____

DICTIONARY WORKOUT

Write each group of words in ABC order.

a b c d e f g h i j k l m n o p q r s t u v w x y z

stack, dog, band

1. _____ 2. _____ 3. _____

last, kiss, sick

4. _____ 5. _____ 6. _____

PROOFREAD

Read the story. Find three words that are not spelled correctly. Write them correctly.

    Beth gott her own breakfast. she had a glass of malk. She had toast with peanut butter and jamm. Then beth ate an orange. her cat had some milk.

1. _____ 2. _____ 3. _____

Now find three words that should begin with capital letters. Write them correctly.

4. _____ 5. _____ 6. _____

1. _____
2. _____
3. _____
4. _____
5. _____
6. _____
7. _____
8. _____
9. _____
10. _____

1. egg
2. fed
3. met
4. yet
5. went
6. nest
7. rest
8. test
9. bend
10. send

pen   mend
mess   west
stem

7 EGG IN A NEST

FOCUS

Say *fed* and *nest*.
Listen for the middle sound.
The middle sound in these
words is called the short *e*
sound.
The sign for short *e* is /e/.
Write *fed* and *nest*.

_____   _____

1. _____   2. _____

Ring the letter that spells the
short *e* sound.

LEARN

Write the core words that rhyme with
the picture names.

(3 words) 1. _____ 2. _____ 3. _____

(2 words) 4. _____ 5. _____

(2 words) 6. _____ 7. _____

(1 word) 8. _____

(1 word) 9. _____

(1 word) 10. _____

CHALLENGE WORDS

Write the challenge word that goes
with each clue. Ring the letter that
spells short *e* in each word.

1. part of a flower   2. something to write with   3. fix clothes

_____   _____   _____

4. not east   5. clean up the ____

_____   _____

PRACTICE

Read the story.
Write the missing core words.

A robin egg lay in the __(1)__. The mother robin sat on the __(2)__ until it hatched. The baby robin __(3)__ its mother. The baby bird could not fly __(4)__. Mother __(5)__ to find food. She came back and __(6)__ the baby a worm.

Read the clues. Write the core word that goes with each clue.

7. _____ a letter

8. not work

9. take a _____

10. a branch can _____

1. _____

2. _____

3. _____

4. _____

5. _____

6. _____

WRITE WORD FAMILIES Add the letters *ed* to make words.

1. b_____

2. sh_____

3. r_____

Add the letters *et* to make words.

4. not dry

w_____

5. fishing _____

n_____

6. your dog or cat

p_____

28

COMMUNICATE

PROOFREAD

Find the spelling mistakes.
Write the words right.

Ed and Meg had robins in their
yard. In the fall the robins wentt
away. Meg and Ed missed the robins.
The snow melted. The robins were
not back yett. Then Meg saw the first
robin of the spring. Meg and Ed
invited Ben and Jenna to see the
nesst.

1. _____

2. _____

3. _____

The names of people begin with a capital letter.
Write the names of four people in the story.
Begin each name with a capital letter.

1. _____ 2. _____ 3. _____ 4. _____

WRITE RIGHT

Cross the letter *t* at the midline.
Write these words.   a rest in the nest

_____

WRITE ON YOUR OWN

Pretend you can fly like a bird. Tell
where you would go. Tell how you
would feel.

29

_____
1. _____

_____
2. _____

_____
3. _____

_____
4. _____

_____
5. _____

_____
6. _____

_____
7. _____

_____
8. _____

_____
9. _____

_____
10. _____

1. us

2. mud

3. rub

4. rug

5. tug

6. luck

7. must

8. rust

9. shut

10. stuck

8 RUB OUT THE MUD!

FOCUS

Say *mud* and *rub*.
Listen for the middle sound.
The middle sound in these
words is called the short *u*
sound.
The sign for short *u* is /u/.
Write *mud* and *rub*.

_____ _____
1. _____ 2. _____

Ring the letter that spells the
short *u* sound in each word.

CHALLENGE

dust   lunch
hush   bunch
rush

30

LEARN

Add the missing letter to make a core word.
Use a letter from the box.

1. | s,b | u__

_ _ _ _ _ _
_____

2. | e,u | l__ck

_ _ _ _ _ _
_____

3. | a,u | r__st

_ _ _ _ _ _
_____

4. | r,f | __ub

_ _ _ _ _ _
_____

5. | k,r | __ug

_ _ _ _ _ _
_____

6. | t,m | shu__

_ _ _ _ _ _
_____

7. | b,d | mu__

_ _ _ _ _ _
_____

8. | m,h | __ust

_ _ _ _ _ _
_____

9. | g,d | tu__

_ _ _ _ _ _
_____

10. | u,e | st__ck

_ _ _ _ _ _
_____

CHALLENGE WORDS

Write the challenge word that fits in
each group of words.

1. breakfast, supper,
_____
_ _ _ _ _ _
_____

2. hurry, run,
_____
_ _ _ _ _ _
_____

3. clean, sweep,
_____
_ _ _ _ _ _
_____

4. shhh! quiet!
_____
_ _ _ _ _ _
_____

5. group, a lot,
_____
_ _ _ _ _ _
_____

Now ring each letter that spells the
short *u* sound.

PRACTICE

Write the core word that fits each clue.

1. You walk on me in the house.

2. I am wet dirt.

3. I am a boat that pulls.

4. I make old cars look ugly.

Write the missing core words.

Don't __(5)__ the wet paint.

The door __(6)__ stay __(7)__.

It is __(8)__.

Bring __(9)__ your old newspapers.

Come to the good __(10)__ store.

1. _____ 2. _____

3. _____ 4. _____

5. _____ 6. _____

7. _____ 8. _____

9. _____ 10. _____

WRITE WORD FAMILIES

Add the letters *ug* to make words.

1. b _ _ _ _   2. h _ _ _   3. m _ _ _ _

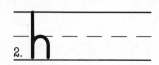

Add the letters *ub* to make words.

4. c _____   5. t _____

32

COMMUNICATE

PROOFREAD

The days of the week begin with capital letters.

Sunday   Monday   Tuesday   Wednesday

Thursday   Friday   Saturday

Write the sentences.

Capitalize the days of the week.

1. Clean the rug on monday.

_____

_____

2. Rub the rust on thursday.

_____

_____

WRITE RIGHT Your short letters should touch the midline.

aceimnorsuvwxz

Write this sentence.

Come with us now.

_____

_____

WRITE ON YOUR OWN

Jessie and Dan washed the family car. Write how they looked when they were done. Write how they felt. Begin days of the week with capital letters.

1. _____
2. _____
3. _____
4. _____
5. _____
6. _____
7. _____
8. _____
9. _____
10. _____

1. drip
2. drum
3. drive
4. drove
5. grin
6. gray
7. grand
8. trip
9. tree
10. truck

9 DRIVE A TRUCK

FOCUS

Say *drive*, *truck*, and *gray*.
Listen for the two beginning sounds.
Write *drive*, *truck*, and *gray*.

1. _____   2. _____

3. _____

Ring the letters in each word that spell the two beginning sounds.

CHALLENGE

dress   grass
trim   grow
try

LEARN

Write the core words that have the
same beginning sounds as the picture
name.

(3 words) 1. _____ 2. _____ 3. _____

(4 words) 4. _____ 5. _____

6. _____ 7. _____

(3 words) 8. _____ 9. _____ 10. _____

CHALLENGE WORDS

Write the challenge word that rhymes
with each clue.

1. him _____   2. slow _____   3. mess _____

4. pass _____   5. by _____

Now ring the letters that spell the
two beginning sounds in each word.

PRACTICE

Write the missing core words.

1. My dad drives a ____.
2. The color of the truck is ____.
3. I think it's a ____ truck.
4. Dad will ____ the truck anywhere.
5. One time he ____ across America.
6. That was a long ____!
7. When he came home, I wanted to beat a ____!
8. Dad had a big ____ on his face. He was happy to be off wheels!

1. _____   2. _____

3. _____   4. _____

5. _____   6. _____

7. _____   8. _____

Write the core word that matches each picture name.

9. _____   10. _____

WRITE WORD FAMILIES

Make the words mean more than one.
Add the letter *s* to the picture names.

1. _____   2. _____   3. _____

4. _____   5. _____   6. _____

COMMUNICATE

DICTIONARY WORKOUT

Which part of the dictionary has the word you need?

Think of the first letter in the word you want to find. Then use this chart.

abcdefghi   jklmnopq   rstuvwxyz

look in the   look in the   look at the
beginning   middle   end

Where would you look for these words in the dictionary? Write *beginning*, *middle*, or *end*.

1. truck _____   2. drip _____   3. mud _____

WRITE RIGHT

Make sure your long letters are not too short. Write each letter 2 times.

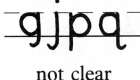
not clear

clear

g   j   p   q

WRITE ON YOUR OWN

Get in the huge gray truck. Where will you go? Write about your trip.

37

1. _____
2. _____
3. _____
4. _____
5. _____
6. _____
7. _____
8. _____
9. _____
10. _____

1. blast
2. blend
3. blink
4. block
5. glad
6. glass
7. plan
8. plot
9. plum
10. plus

10 GLAD TO BLAST OFF!

FOCUS

Say *blast*, *glad*, and *plum*.
Listen for the two beginning
sounds.
Write *blast*, *glad*, and *plum*.

1. _____   2. _____

3. _____

Ring the letters in each word
that spell the two beginning
sounds.

blank   glue
blanket   gloves
planet

38

LEARN Write the core words that have the same beginning sounds as the picture word.

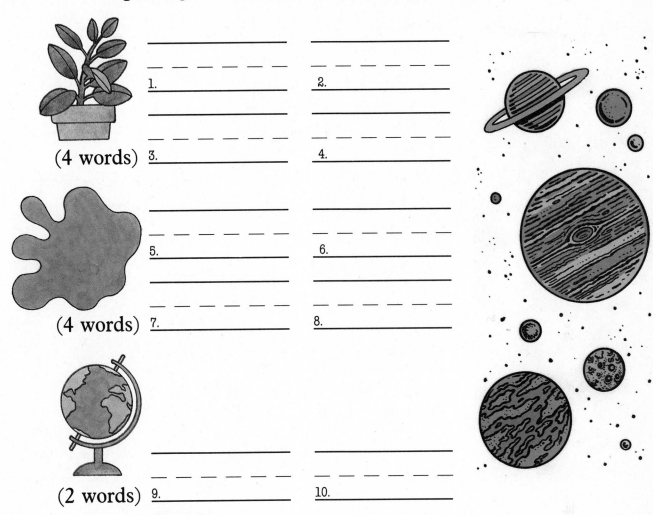

(4 words) 1. _____ 2. _____
3. _____ 4. _____

(4 words) 5. _____ 6. _____
7. _____ 8. _____

(2 words) 9. _____ 10. _____

CHALLENGE WORDS Write the challenge word that fits each clue.

1. keeps you warm
_____

2. something sticky
_____

3. mittens or _____
_____

4. Earth or Mars
_____

5. fill in the _____
_____

Now ring the letters that spell the
two beginning sounds in each word.

PRACTICE

Write the missing core words.

I feel __(1)__ when July 4th comes.
Everyone on our __(2)__ has a picnic. I
drink one __(3)__ of cold juice after
another. Our town has a fireworks
show. We watch them __(4)__ off. They
are gone before you can __(5)__ your
eyes. Fireworks __(6)__ a picnic equals
a good time for me.

Write the core word that goes with
each clue.

7. This is a purple fruit.   8. This is a small piece of land.

9. Think ahead.   10. Mix together.

1. _____ 2. _____

3. _____ 4. _____

5. _____ 6. _____

7. _____ 8. _____

9. _____ 10. _____

WRITE WORD FAMILIES

Solve these word math problems.
Write the new words.
Ring the word that names the picture.

1. plot − pl + bl = _____

2. plum − pl + gl = _____

3. glass − gl + gr = _____

4. plot − pl + tr = _____

5. plum − pl + dr = _____

COMMUNICATE

blast
blend
blink
block
glad
glass
plan
plot
plum
plus

PROOFREAD

The names of special days begin with capital letters.

Thanksgiving   Halloween   Valentine's Day

Write the sentences.

Capitalize the names of special days.

1. I am glad on halloween.

_____

- -

_____

2. Eat plums on thanksgiving.

_____

- -

WRITE RIGHT

Trace over your first line when you make these letters.

Write this sentence.

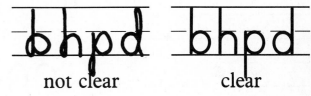

not clear   clear

I plan the birthday party.

_____

- -

WRITE ON YOUR OWN

Prepare for take-off. You are the astronaut! Write how you feel! Write what you do. Write *b*, *h*, *p*, and *d* clearly.

41

1. _____
2. _____
3. _____
4. _____
5. _____
6. _____
7. _____
8. _____
9. _____
10. _____

CORE

1. ask
2. desk
3. mask
4. camp
5. dump
6. jump
7. long
8. song
9. sting
10. wing

FOCUS

Say *mask*, *camp*, and *song*.
Listen for the ending sounds.
Write *mask*, *camp*, and *song*.

1. _____   2. _____

3. _____

Ring the two letters in each
word that spell the ending
sounds.

CHALLENGE

blimp   bring
grump   task
stamp

42

LEARN Name the picture.

Write the core words that have the same ending sound or sounds as the picture name.

(4 words)

1. _____ 2. _____ 3. _____

4. _____

(3 words)

5. _____ 6. _____ 7. _____

Read the picture word.
Write the three core words that have the
same ending sounds as the picture name.

husk (3 words)

8. _____ 9. _____ 10. _____

CHALLENGE WORDS Write the challenge word that fits each clue.

1. a job
_____

2. carry
_____

3. an air ship
_____

4. goes on a letter
_____

5. sulk or fuss
_____

Ring the letters that spell the ending
sounds in these words.

PRACTICE   Write the missing core words.

When you __(1)__ in the woods, remember these things. Be sure to __(2)__ someone where you can put your tent. Bugs may __(3)__, so bring a spray. Take a __(4)__ walk and look for birds. Sing a happy camp __(5)__. Before you leave, __(6)__ your trash in a trash can.

Write the core word that names the picture.

7.

8.

9.

10.

1. _____   2. _____

3. _____   4. _____

5. _____   6. _____

7. _____   8. _____

9. _____   10. _____

WRITE WORD FAMILIES   Write the words that mean more than one. Use the letter s at the end of each word.

1. _____

2. _____

3. _____

4. _____

5. _____

COMMUNICATE
DICTIONARY WORKOUT

a b c d e f g h i   j k l m n o p q   r s t u v w x y z

beginning   middle   end

ask
desk
mask
camp
dump
jump
long
song
sting
wing

Where would you look for these words in the dictionary? Write *beginning*, *middle*, or *end*.

1. song
   _____
   _ _ _ _ _ _ _ _
   _____

2. long
   _____
   _ _ _ _ _ _ _ _
   _____

3. jump
   _____
   _ _ _ _ _ _ _ _
   _____

4. wing
   _____
   _ _ _ _ _ _ _ _
   _____

5. desk
   _____
   _ _ _ _ _ _ _ _
   _____

WRITE RIGHT   Space your letters evenly.

camping   camping   camping

too close together   too far apart   clear

Write this sentence.   Let's sing a camp song.

WRITE ON YOUR OWN

You are inside the tent. It's a dark night in the woods. You hear sounds outside. Write about what you hear. Write about how you feel.

45

UNIT **7**

Remember the short *e* sound as in *let*.

Find the missing letter. Then write the words.

egg
bend
nest
sent
yet
rest

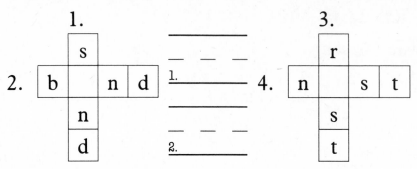

1.

	s			
2. b		n	d	
	n			
	d			

1. _____

_____

2. _____

3.

	r			
4. n		s	t	
	s			
	t			

3. _____

_____

4. _____

Write the word that rhymes with each word.

5. leg _____   6. net _____

FOCUS   Ring the letter that spells the short *e*
sound in each word.

UNIT **8**

Remember the short *u* sound as in *cut*.

Write the three rhyming pairs of words.

luck
rug
stuck
must
rust
tug

1. _____   2. _____

3. _____   4. _____

5. _____   6. _____

FOCUS   Ring the letter that spells the short *u*
sound in each word.

UNIT 9

grand
drive
drip
gray
trip
drove

Remember the *dr* in *dress*,
the *tr* in *try*, and the *gr* in *grow*.
Write the two word pairs with the
same ending sounds.

_____   _____

1. _____   2. _____

_____   _____

3. _____   4. _____

Write the word that rhymes with each word.

_____   _____

day   5. _____   sand   6. _____

FOCUS   Ring the two letters that spell the
beginning sounds in each word.

UNIT 10

glad
plum
glass
block
blend
plus

Remember the *bl* in *blue,*
the *gl* in *glue,* and the *pl* in *please.*
Write the word that rhymes with each word.

1. pass   2. lock   3. bus

_____   _____   _____

_____   _____   _____

4. end   5. gum   6. sad

_____   _____   _____

_____   _____   _____

FOCUS   Ring the two letters that spell the
beginning sounds in each word.

47

Remember the *mp* in *stamp*,
the *sk* in *task*, and the *ng* in *sing*.
Write the three word pairs that
rhyme.

dump
long
jump
mask
ask
song

1. _____ 2. _____

3. _____ 4. _____

5. _____ 6. _____

FOCUS

Ring the two letters that spell the
ending sounds in each word.

WRITE WORD FAMILIES

Drop the first letter of each word.
Write the new words.

1. nest b_____ 2. luck d_____

3. tug b_____ 4. jump b_____

Drop the first two letters of each
word. Write the new words.

5. drip sk_____ 6. plum dr_____

48

DICTIONARY WORKOUT

Remember that words in a dictionary are in ABC order. Write *beginning,* *middle,* or *end* to tell where you would look for these words in a dictionary.

a b c d e f g h i
beginning

j k l m n o p q
middle

r s t u v w x y z
end

1. yet _____

_ _ _ _ _ _ _

_____

2. drip _____

_ _ _ _ _ _ _

_____

3. must _____

_ _ _ _ _ _ _

_____

PROOFREAD

Read the story. Find three words that are not spelled correctly. Write them correctly.

It is not halloween yett. Halloween will come next tuesday. I will be gladd then! I think october is a grend month because it has Halloween!

_____   _____   _____

_ _ _ _ _ _   _ _ _ _ _ _   _ _ _ _ _ _

1. _____   2. _____   3. _____

Now find three words that should begin with capital letters. Write them correctly.

_____   _____   _____

_ _ _ _ _ _   _ _ _ _ _ _   _ _ _ _ _ _

4. _____   5. _____   6. _____

49

1. _____
2. _____
3. _____
4. _____
5. _____
6. _____
7. _____
8. _____
9. _____
10. _____

CORE

1. **came**
2. **cane**
3. **rake**
4. **grape**
5. **plate**
6. **pail**
7. **bait**
8. **raise**
9. **hay**
10. **say**

CHALLENGE

aid   stain
pain   blaze
trail

FOCUS

Say *came*, *pail*, and *hay*.
Listen for the vowel sound in
each word.
This vowel sound is called
long *a*. The sign for long *a*
is /ā/. The letters *a-e*, *ai*, and *ay*
spell long *a*.
Write *came*, *pail*, and *hay*.

1. _____   2. _____

3. _____

Ring the two letters in each
word that spell the long *a*
sound.

50

LEARN

The long *a* sound may be spelled *ay*.
Write two core words that rhyme
with the picture name.

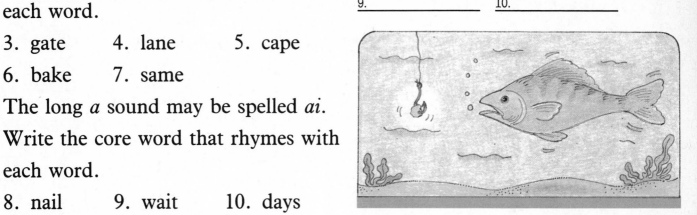

1-2. tray

The long *a* sound may be spelled *a-e*
as in *bake*.

Write the core word that rhymes with
each word.

3. gate   4. lane   5. cape

6. bake   7. same

The long *a* sound may be spelled *ai*.
Write the core word that rhymes with
each word.

8. nail   9. wait   10. days

1. _____   2. _____

3. _____   4. _____

5. _____   6. _____

7. _____   8. _____

9. _____   10. _____

CHALLENGE WORDS   Write the challenge word that fits each clue.

1. You hike on it.   2. It's dirty.   3. It hurts.

_____   _____   _____

4. It's a help.   5. It's a fire.

_____   _____

Ring the letters that spell long *a* in
each word.

51

PRACTICE

Write the missing core words.

I fish with a long ___(1)___ pole.
Worms are the ___(2)___ I use. Some days
I have no fish to carry home in my
___(3)___. But I'd ___(4)___ that I'm lucky
most of the time. When I ___(5)___ my
line out of the water, a fish is usually
on the hook. One day I ___(6)___ home
with ten fish! At supper, two fresh
fish were on each ___(7)___. Yum!

Write the core word that names the
picture.

1. _____ 2. _____

3. _____ 4. _____

5. _____ 6. _____

7. _____ 8. _____

9. _____ 10. _____

8.  9. 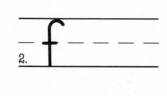 10.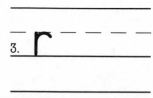

WRITE WORD FAMILIES

Add the letters *ail* to make words.
Then ring the word that names the
picture.

1. h _____ 2. f _____ 3. r _____

4. m _____ 5. t _____ 6. s _____

52

COMMUNICATE

PROOFREAD

A sentence that tells something ends
with a period (.).
Write the sentences.
Add the correct punctuation mark at
the end.

Dad came fishing with me

1.

We took bait in a pail

2.

came

cane

rake

grape

plate

pail

bait

raise

hay

say

WRITE RIGHT

All capital letters touch the top line.
Write each capital letter once.

ABCDEFGHIJKLMNOPQRSTUVWXYZ

WRITE ON YOUR OWN

"The fish I caught was so big that its
fin was used as a ship's sail." That is
a fish story. Write your own fish story.
Tell about the huge fish you caught.

53

1. _____

2. _____

3. _____

4. _____

5. _____

6. _____

7. _____

8. _____

9. _____

10. _____

CORE

1. bean
2. meal
3. team
4. each
5. dream
6. treat
7. deep
8. seen
9. sheep
10. wheel

CHALLENGE

mean   sleep
leave   sneeze
cream

FOCUS

Say *bean* and *seen*.
Listen for the middle sound.
This vowel sound is called long *e*.
The sign for long *e* is /ē/.
Write *bean* and *seen*.

1. _____   2. _____

Ring the two letters in each
word that spell the long *e* sound.

LEARN

Write the core words that rhyme.
Ring the letters that spell /ē/.

1. heel _____

2. green _____

3. peep _____

4. keep _____

Write the core words that rhyme.
Ring the letters that spell /ē/.

5. cream _____

6. scream _____

7. peach _____

8. meat _____

9. lean _____

10. real _____

CHALLENGE WORDS

Write a challenge word that means
the opposite.

1. come _____

2. wake _____

Write a challenge word that rhymes.

3. bean _____

4. bees _____

5. dream _____

Ring the letters that spell long *e* in
each word.

PRACTICE

Write the missing core words.

Last night I fell into a __(1)__ sleep. Then I had a strange __(2)__.

I dreamed about a boy who watched over a herd of __(3)__. The boy was poor. He had only four beans to eat for his __(4)__. But the boy got a wonderful __(5)__. He found out that __(6)__ bean was magic! Each little __(7)__ turned into something else. Each bean turned into a __(8)__ that went around and around! On top of the wheels was a beautiful coach! The coach was pulled by a __(9)__ of white horses! The boy rode into the sky, laughing. He was never __(10)__ again.

1. _____
2. _____
3. _____
4. _____
5. _____
6. _____
7. _____
8. _____
9. _____
10. _____

WRITE WORD FAMILIES

Add the letters *eat* to make words.

1. b_____
2. h_____
3. m_____

Add the letters *eal* to make words.

4. s_____
5. d_____
6. h_____

Now ring the word that names each picture.

56

COMMUNICATE

PROOFREAD

A sentence that asks a question ends
in a question mark (?).
Write the sentences.
Add the correct punctuation mark at
the end.

1. Did you dream

_____

- -

_____

2. What did you dream about

_____

- -

_____

CORE WORDS

bean
meal
team
each
dream
treat
deep
seen
sheep
wheel

WRITE RIGHT

Small *t* does not touch the top line.

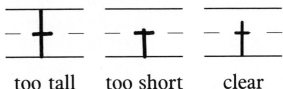

too tall   too short   clear

Write the word *treat*. Write each *t* clearly.

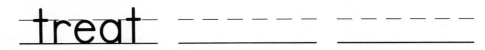

treat

WRITE ON YOUR OWN

You are going to sleep in this bed.
Write about a dream you have. Sweet
dreams! Check your punctuation.

57

15 FLY OUT OF SIGHT

CORE

1. _____

2. _____

3. _____

4. _____

5. _____

6. _____

7. _____

8. _____

9. _____

10. _____

1. pine
2. wide
3. fly
4. dry
5. shy
6. fight
7. light
8. night
9. right
10. sight

FOCUS

Say *pine*, *fly*, and *night*.
Listen for the vowel sound in
each word.
This vowel sound is called
long *i*.
The sign for long *i* is /ī/.
Write *pine*, *fly*, and *night*.

1. _____   2. _____

3. _____

Ring the letter or letters that
spell the long *i* sound in each
word.

CHALLENGE

might   sly

tight   cry

stripe

58

LEARN

Say each picture name.
Write the core words that rhyme with it.

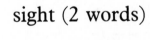

_____   _____   _____

1. _____   2. _____   3. _____

_____   _____

(5 words)   4. _____   5. _____

_____   _____   _____

(3 words)   6. _____   7. _____   8. _____

Write the core words that rhyme.

_____   _____

nine (1 word)   9. _____   slide (1 word)   10. _____

CHALLENGE WORDS ;

Read each core word below. Write
the challenge word or words that have
the same spelling of /ī/.

_____   _____

sight (2 words)   1. _____   2. _____

_____   _____

shy (2 words)   3. _____   4. _____

_____

wide (1 word)   5. _____

PRACTICE

Write the missing core words.

An airplane can ___(1)___ . It can fly at ___(2)___ in the dark. It can fly during the day when there's ___(3)___ from the sun. The first airplane was a wonderful ___(4)___ to see! The Wright brothers flew that plane ___(5)___ over the sandy beach!

Write the word for each clue.

6. not bold or outgoing
7. not narrow or thin
8. not wet
9. try not to ____ with each other
10. a kind of tree

1. _____   2. _____

3. _____   4. _____

5. _____   6. _____

7. _____   8. _____

9. _____   10. _____

WRITE WORD FAMILIES

Add the letters *ine* to make words.

1. m_____   2. f_____   3. l_____

Add the letters *ide* to make words.

4. h_____   5. s_____   6. r_____

Ring the word that names the picture.

COMMUNICATE

DICTIONARY WORKOUT

Many words have more than one meaning.

A dictionary lists all the meanings for a word.

Read the pairs of meanings.

Write the core word that fits *both* meanings.

1. a. an insect with two wings
   b. move through the air

   1. _____

2. a. a lamp
   b. not heavy

   2. _____

WRITE RIGHT

Some capital letters and small letters look almost the same. But they are different in some ways.

Write each pair of letters.

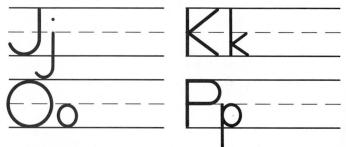

Jj   Kk
Oo   Pp

WRITE ON YOUR OWN

You're flying in a plane. Write what you see out the window. Write how the world looks far below.

61

MY SNOW COAT

1. _____

2. _____

3. _____

4. _____

5. _____

6. _____

7. _____

8. _____

9. _____

10. _____

1. poke

2. boat

3. coat

4. goat

5. soap

6. toad

7. row

8. blow

9. snow

10. tow

FOCUS

Say *poke*, *goat*, and *blow*.
Listen for the vowel sound in each word.
This vowel sound is called long *o*.
The sign for long *o* is /ō/.
Write *poke*, *goat*, and *blow*.

1. _____   2. _____

3. _____

Ring the two letters in each word that spell the long *o* sound.

CHALLENGE

coach   slow

float   globe

toast

LEARN

Write four core words that rhyme with *low*.
Ring the letters that spell /ō/.

_____ _____ _____ _____

1. _____ 2. _____ 3. _____ 4. _____

Write the core word that rhymes with *joke*.
Ring the letters that spell /ō/.

_____

5. _____

Write the core words that rhyme with each
picture word.
Ring the letters that spell /ō/.

(3 words)   6. _____   7. _____   8. _____

(1 word)   9. _____   (1 word)   10. _____

CHALLENGE WORDS   Read each core word below. Write
the challenge word or words that have
the same spelling of /ō/.

_____ _____ _____

soap (3 words)   1. _____   2. _____   3. _____

blow (1 word)   4. _____   poke (1 word)   5. _____

PRACTICE

Write the missing core words.

1. This animal is a mountain ____.
2. It has a thick ____ of fur to keep it warm.
3. Ice and ____ will often cover the rocks of its home.
4. A cold wind will often ____.
5. The mountain goat has to ____ its nose around to find plants to eat.

Write the core word that fits each clue.

6. an animal like a frog
7. to pull a boat
8. something to wash with

Write the missing core words in the song.
"Row, __(9)__, row your __(10)__ gently down the stream."

1. _____
2. _____
3. _____
4. _____
5. _____
6. _____
7. _____
8. _____
9. _____
10. _____

WRITE WORD FAMILIES

Work out the "Word Math." Write the new words. Ring the word that names the picture.

1. tow − t + cr = _____

2. row − r + l = _____

3. toad − t + r = _____

4. coat − t + l = _____

64

COMMUNICATE

PROOFREAD

A sentence that shows surprise or strong
feeling ends with an exclamation point (!).
Write the sentences.
Add the correct punctuation mark at the end.

1. Look at all the snow

_____

_ _

_____

2. What a surprise

_____

_ _

_____

WRITE RIGHT

Some capital letters and small letters
look almost the same. Study how
these letter pairs are alike and different.
Write these names.

Cecil Susan Ursula

_____   _____   _____

_ _ _ _ _ _ _ _   _ _ _ _ _ _ _ _   _ _ _ _ _ _ _ _

_____   _____   _____

WRITE ON YOUR OWN

You helped to make a snowman.
Write its name. Write one thing it
likes to do. Try to make all your
letters so they are easy to read.

CORE

1. _____

2. _____

3. _____

4. _____

5. _____

6. _____

7. _____

8. _____

9. _____

10. _____

1. tune

2. rude

3. tube

4. zoo

5. soon

6. moon

7. boot

8. food

9. pool

10. room

FOCUS

Say *tune* and *zoo*.
Listen for the vowel sound in each word.
The sign for this vowel sound is /ü/.
Write *tune* and *zoo*.

1. _____   2. _____

Ring the two letters in each word that spell the sound /ü/.

CHALLENGE

moose   balloon

goose   shoot

zoom

66

LEARN

Read the clue words.

Write the *oo* words that rhyme.

root, toot, (1)
noon, spoon, (2) , (3)
spool, fool, (4)
moo, (5)
mood, (6)
boom, zoom, (7)

Write the core word that has the same ending sound as each picture word.

1. _____ 2. _____

3. _____ 4. _____

5. _____ 6. _____

7. _____ 8. _____

9. _____ 10. _____

8.

9.

10.

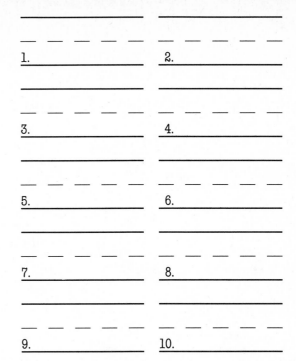

CHALLENGE WORDS

Write the challenge words that fit the clues.

1. blow this up
_____

2. rhymes with *room*
_____

3. large bird
_____

4. animal in deer family
_____

5. do this with a basketball
_____

PRACTICE

Write the core word that goes with each clue.

1. You swim in it.
2. not polite
3. You eat it.
4. It holds toothpaste.
5. You sing it.
6. You see it at night.
7. It goes on a foot.
8. part of a house
9. Animals live there.
10. not a long time

1.	2.
3.	4.
5.	6.
7.	8.
9.	10.

WRITE WORD FAMILIES

Add the letters *ool* to make words.

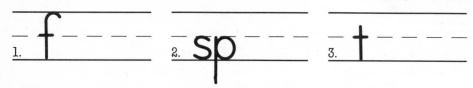

1. f   2. sp   3. t

Add the letters *oom* to make words.

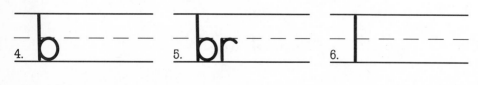

4. b   5. br   6. l

Ring the word that names the picture.

68

COMMUNICATE

DICTIONARY WORKOUT

Many words have more than one meaning. A dictionary lists all the meanings for a word. Read the two different meanings for the word *room*. Write the letter of the meaning that shows how *room* is used in each sentence.

a. part of a building with walls of its own

b. space

1. Is there *room* for me on the bench?

2. A kitchen is the *room* for cooking.

1. _____   2. _____

WRITE RIGHT

Some capital and small letters look quite alike.

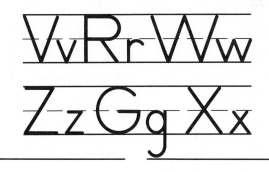

Study these letter pairs. Write the four letter pairs that have capital and small letters that are quite alike.

1. _____   2. _____   3. _____   4. _____

WRITE ON YOUR OWN

Write a question for this zoo animal. Make believe it can talk back! Write its answer to your question.

69

Remember the long *a* sound as in *day*. Find the missing letters. Then write the words.

grape
say
hay
cane
raise
pail

1. h____ _____

2. c__n__ _____

3. p____l _____

4. gr__p__ _____

5. r____s__ _____

6. s____ _____

FOCUS Ring the two letters that spell the long *a* sound in each word.

Remember the long *e* sound as in *me*. Write the word pairs that rhyme.

meal
dream
wheel
deep
team
sheep

keep   1._____   2._____

seem   3._____   4._____

feel   5._____   6._____

FOCUS Ring the two letters that spell the long *e* sound in each word.

UNIT 15

Remember the long *i* sound as in *my*.
Find the missing letters. Write the words.

wide
right
fly
night
light
sight

1.
| l |
| |
| |
| |

3.
| r |
| |
| |

2. n | | | | t   4. s | | | t

1. _____
2. _____
3. _____
4. _____

Write the word that rhymes with each word.

5. side _____   6. sly _____

FOCUS Ring the letter or letters that spell the long *i* sound in each word.

UNIT 16

Remember the long *o* sound as in *slow*.
Put the letters in order. Write the words.

poke
snow
row
boat
blow
goat

1. pkoe _____   2. owbl _____

3. snwo _____   4. btoa _____

5. tgoa _____   6. wor _____

FOCUS

Ring the two letters that spell the
long *o* sound in each word.

71

Remember the /ü/ as in *shoot*.
Name the picture. Write the
words that have the same ending
sound.

food

moon

soon

tube

tune

rude

_____
1. _____

_____
2. _____

_____
3. _____

_____
4. _____

_____
5. _____

_____
6. _____

FOCUS

Ring the two letters that spell /ü/ in
each word.

WRITE WORD FAMILIES

Do the Word Math. Write the new words.

1. pail − p + h = _____

2. deep − d + p = _____

3. wide − d + s = _____

4. poke − k + l = _____

Remember that adding the ending *s*
makes a word mean more than one.
Write these words so they mean more
than one.

5. boot _____

6. tune _____

DICTIONARY WORKOUT

Remember that a word may have
more than one meaning. Read the
different meanings for the underlined
words. Write the letter of the
meaning that shows how the word is
used in each sentence.

raise. **a.** lift up. **b.** higher pay.

1. _____ Mom was pleased to get a <u>raise</u> at work.

2. _____ <u>Raise</u> your hand if you know the answer.

right. **a.** correct. **b.** opposite of left.

1. _____ Who knows the <u>right</u> answer?

2. _____ Most people write with their <u>right</u> hand.

PROOFREAD

Write the punctuation mark that
belongs in each blue circle. Use these: **. ! ?**
1. Help, the goat got out◯
2. How did that happen◯
3. There's no time to talk now◯

1. ◯ 2. ◯ 3. ◯

CORE

1. _____
2. _____
3. _____
4. _____
5. _____
6. _____
7. _____
8. _____
9. _____
10. _____

1. what
2. why
3. where
4. while
5. clash
6. flash
7. shame
8. shine
9. shock
10. shore

19
WHAT A CLASH!

FOCUS

Say *what* and *shine*.
Listen to the beginning sound.
Write *what* and *shine*.

1. _____ 2. _____

Ring the two letters that spell the beginning sound in each word.
Say *clash*.
Listen to the ending sound.
Write *clash*.

3. _____

Ring the two letters that spell the ending sound.

CHALLENGE

shall   whisper
share   whiskers
shadow

74

LEARN

Write the core words that have the same beginning sound as the picture name.

_____   _____   _____   _____

1. _____   2. _____   3. _____   4. _____

Write the core words that have the same beginning sound as the picture name.

_____   _____   _____   _____

5. _____   6. _____   7. _____   8. _____

Write the core words that have the same ending sound as the picture name.

_____   _____

9. _____   10. _____

CHALLENGE WORDS

Write the missing challenge words. Ring the two letters that spell the beginning sound.

1. The cat is as quiet as a _____.
2. It comes to _____ my dinner!
3. I _____ feed the cat some of my fish.
4. It will eat in the _____ of the table.
5. Then the cat will wash its _____.

_____   _____   _____

1. _____   2. _____   3. _____

_____   _____

4. _____   5. _____

PRACTICE

Write the missing core words.

Can you guess __(1)__ I play in the band? Because I love to hear the __(2)__ of brass! Last week, I played __(3)__ our band marched. The place __(4)__ we marched was fun. We marched along the __(5)__ of a lake!

At first, the day was nice. We hoped the sun would __(6)__. But do you know __(7)__ happened? Suddenly it grew dark! There was a __(8)__ of light! Thunder roared! The storm came as a __(9)__ to all of us. It was a __(10)__ that we got all wet. But I had fun clashing along with the thunder!

1. _____ 2. _____

3. _____ 4. _____

5. _____ 6. _____

7. _____ 8. _____

9. _____ 10. _____

WRITE WORD FAMILIES Make words.

Add a letter from the box to the beginning of the word.

| m | c | l | bl |

1. ash   2. ash   3. ash

4. ame   5. ame   6. ame

76

COMMUNICATE
DICTIONARY WORKOUT

An entry word is the word you look up in a dictionary. A definition tells you what the word means. Many entry words have more than one definition. Look at this entry.

> **shine** /shīn/   **1** *v.* send out light.   **2** *v.* polish.   **3** *n.* fair weather.   **4** *v.* be bright.

1. What is the entry word? _____

2. How many definitions does it have? _____

3. What is the second definition? _____

WRITE RIGHT   Write the letters *e* and *f* so they are easy to read.

not clear    clear

Write each letter three times.

e _____   f _____

WRITE ON YOUR OWN

Write the words to your favorite song. Then make up a new line for it. Write the letters *e* and *f* so they are easy to read.

CORE WORDS

what
why
where
while
clash
flash
shame
shine
shock
shore

77

20 A MISSING TOOTH

1. _____
2. _____
3. _____
4. _____
5. _____
6. _____
7. _____
8. _____
9. _____
10. _____

1. much
2. peach
3. teach
4. chick
5. choke
6. bath
7. with
8. tooth
9. thin
10. thank

FOCUS

Say *chick* and *thin*.
Listen to the beginning sound.
Write *chick* and *thin*.

1. _____ 2. _____

Ring the two letters that spell the beginning sound in each word.
Say *teach* and *tooth*.
Listen to the ending sound.
Write *teach* and *tooth*.

3. _____ 4. _____

Ring the two letters that spell the ending sound in each word.

CHALLENGE

child   thick
chore   think
reach

LEARN

Find the missing letters for the words below. Write the words.

1. tea _ _   2. pea _ _   3. mu _ _

4. _ _ oke   5. _ _ ick

Write the word that rhymes with each dark word.

6. Please ride ____ Mr. **Smith.**

7. Do your **math,** then take a ____.

8. Do ____ Uncle **Hank.**

9. It's as ____ as a **pin.**

10. She lost a ____; that's the **truth!**

1. _____ 2. _____

3. _____ 4. _____

5. _____ 6. _____

7. _____ 8. _____

9. _____ 10. _____

CHALLENGE WORDS

Write two challenge words that have the same beginning sound as *thank.*

1. _____ 2. _____

Write two challenge words that have the same beginning sound as *choke.*

3. _____ 4. _____

Write the challenge word that has the same ending sound as *teach.*

5. _____

79

PRACTICE

Write the missing core words.

One Monday, I woke up __(1)__ all my teeth. At breakfast I ate a golden __(2)__. Out fell my front __(3)__!

"There's so __(4)__ I can do with this tooth," I said. "First I'll give it a __(5)__ to make it clean. Then I'll . . ."

I couldn't think of anything else to do with my tooth. "Do you want it, Mom?" I asked.

"Yes, __(6)__ you." she said. And that was the end of that.

1. _____ 2. _____

3. _____ 4. _____

5. _____ 6. _____

7. _____ 8. _____

9. _____ 10. _____

Read the clues to the missing core words. Write the words.

It's not fat and not __(9)__.

A mother hen has a baby __(7)__.
To help to learn is to __(8)__.
Smoke can make you __(10)__.

WRITE WORD FAMILIES

Add the letters *ick* to make words.

1. w 2. st 3. br

Add the letters *ank* to make words.

4. b 5. sp 6. cr

Now ring the words that name the pictures.

SAVE YOUR
MONEY HERE

COMMUNICATE
PROOFREAD

Write the punctuation mark that belongs in the blue circle at the end of each sentence. Use one of these punctuation marks: . ! ?

1. Where is the little yellow chick ◯
2. I don't see it ◯
3. Is it with the pigs ◯
4. Oh, no ◯
5. The chick is in the mud ◯
6. The yellow chick is black now ◯
7. What a mess ◯

1. ◯   2. ◯   3. ◯   4. ◯
5. ◯   6. ◯   7. ◯

WRITE RIGHT

Do not write your punctuation marks too lightly.
Make them dark enough to be seen.
Write these sentences.   Watch out! Who, me? Yes.

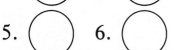

WRITE ON YOUR OWN

Tell about a time when you lost a tooth. Be sure to tell how it came out. Tell how it felt and what you did with it, too. Write the right punctuation mark at the end of each sentence.

81

CORE

_____
1. _____

_____
2. _____

_____
3. _____

_____
4. _____

_____
5. _____

_____
6. _____

_____
7. _____

_____
8. _____

_____
9. _____

_____
10. _____

1. art

2. cart

3. barn

4. farm

5. hard

6. yard

7. dark

8. park

9. shark

10. sharp

FOCUS

Say *barn* and *farm*.
Listen to the middle sound in each word.
The sign for this sound is /är/.
Write *barn* and *farm*.

_____ _____
1. _____ 2. _____

Ring the two letters that spell the middle sound in each word.

CHALLENGE

harm   march

alarm   smart

arms

LEARN Use the letters *ar* to spell /är/.

Write the core word that rhymes with
arm.

1. _____

Write three core words that rhyme
with *ark*.

2. _____   3. _____   4. _____

Write the core words that rhyme with
the picture names.

5. (1 word) _____

6. (1 word) _____

7. (2 words) _____   _____

8. (2 words) _____   _____

CHALLENGE WORDS Write the missing challenge words.
Ring the letters that spell /är/.

Firefighters have to be __(1)__ and
fast. When the __(2)__ sounds, they go
in a hurry. They don't have time to
__(3)__. They run! They work hard to
save people from __(4)__. Sometimes
they carry people out of a burning
building in their __(5)__.

1. _____   2. _____

3. _____   4. _____

5. _____

PRACTICE

Write the missing core words.

  My friend Mark lives on a __(1)__.
Like most farmers, Mark works
__(2)__. Every night, he fills a __(3)__
with feed for the pigs. Then he goes
to the __(4)__ to milk the cows.
Sometimes, Mark works until it's
__(5)__ outside.

Read the word meanings. Write the
core word that fits each meaning.

6. an outside place for rest or play
7. a large fish
8. drawings and paintings
9. the ground around a house or
   school
10. able to cut

1. _____   2. _____

3. _____   4. _____

5. _____   6. _____

7. _____   8. _____

9. _____   10. _____

WRITE WORD FAMILIES

Make each word mean more than
one.

Add the letter *s* to each word.

1. cart _____   2. shark _____   3. barn _____

4. farm _____   5. park _____

COMMUNICATE

DICTIONARY WORKOUT

The meanings of some words are easier to understand by seeing a picture. That's why the dictionary gives pictures for some words. The picture is called an illustration. Beside every illustration is the name of the entry word and the number of the definition.

CORE WORDS

art
cart
barn
farm
hard
yard
dark
park
shark
sharp

 **park** /pärk/   1 *n* an open space for everyone.   2 *v* to leave a car for a time.

1. Write the entry word that has an illustration.
2. Write the number of the definition that the picture shows.

_____ _____
_ _ _ _ _ _ _ _ _ _ _ _
1._____ 2._____

WRITE RIGHT

Leave the right amount of space between your words. This makes them easy to read. Write the words.   the farm

_____
_ _ _ _ _ _ _ _ _ _ _ _
_____

WRITE ON YOUR OWN

Give the cow a name. Write a make-believe story about what she likes to do.

85

MY HORSE IS FIRST!

1. _____
2. _____
3. _____
4. _____
5. _____
6. _____
7. _____
8. _____
9. _____
10. _____

1. bird
2. girl
3. dirt
4. shirt
5. first
6. for
7. more
8. horn
9. horse
10. short

FOCUS

Say *horse*.

Listen for the middle sound.

Write *horse*.

_____

1. _____

Ring the two letters that spell the middle sound.

Say *first*.

Listen for the middle sound.

The sign for this sound is /ėr/.

Write *first*.

_____

2. _____

Ring the two letters that spell the middle sound.

CHALLENGE

store   third

morning   whirl

dinosaur

LEARN

Write the core words that complete each puzzle. Use words that have the sounds of *or*.

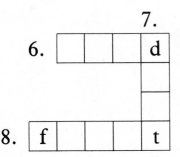

2. | s | h | | | t |
3. | m | | | e |

1. h (vertical)

4. h (vertical)
5. | f | |
   n (vertical)

Use words in which /ėr/ is spelled *ir* as in *sir*.

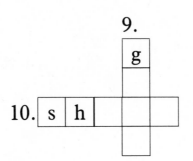

6. | | | | d |
7. d (vertical)
8. | f | | | t |

9. g (vertical)
10. | s | h | | |

___ 1. ___ 2.

___ 3. ___ 4.

___ 5. ___ 6.

___ 7. ___ 8.

___ 9. ___ 10.

CHALLENGE WORDS

Write the challenge word that fits each clue. Ring the letters that spell /ėr/ and the sounds of *or*.

1. It comes after *second*.
2. You can buy things there.
3. It's the beginning of the day.
4. It's what spinning tops do.
5. It's an animal that lived long ago.

___ 1. ___ 2. ___ 3.

___ 4. ___ 5.

87

PRACTICE

Write the core word that is missing in each sentence.

1. I like my __(1)__ to gallop.
2. This is a present __(2)__ Mom.

Write the core words that name the pictures.

3.  4.  5.

6.   7.

Write the core words that mean the opposite.

8. last 9. tall 10. less

1. _____ 2. _____

3. _____ 4. _____

5. _____ 6. _____

7. _____ 8. _____

9. _____ 10. _____

WRITE WORD FAMILIES

Make the words mean more than one.
Add the letter *s* to each word.

1. shirt   2. bird   3. horse

   2   5   10

4. horn   5. girl

   8   twin

88

COMMUNICATE

PROOFREAD

Find the spelling mistakes. Write
each sentence with the right words.
Add one of these punctuation marks
at the end: . ! ?

1. Three cheers fer my horse
2. Did it come in firss
3. Yes, my hoars won

1. _____

2. _____

3. _____

WRITE RIGHT

Practice writing the letters *o, i,* and *r.*
Write them so they will be easy to read.
Write the words   short girl.

o   i   r

WRITE ON YOUR OWN

Which horse will win the race? Make
up a name for it. Tell how it wins.

89

1. _____

2. _____

3. _____

4. _____

5. _____

6. _____

7. _____

8. _____

9. _____

10. _____

CHALLENGE

any   find

away   kind

goes

CORE

1. does

2. were

3. every

4. very

5. give

6. live

7. thing

8. your

9. many

10. who

23 WHO RUNS MANY MILES?

FOCUS

Some words are not spelled as they sound.

You must remember the letters that spell these words.

The words *who* and *many* are not spelled as they sound.

Say *who* and *many*.

Write the words.

_____   _____

1. _____   2. _____

LEARN

Write the core word that rhymes with
each word below.

1. fur _____   2. poor _____   3. fuzz _____

4. ring _____   5. do _____

Write three core words that end with
the letter *y*.

6. _____   7. _____   8. _____

Write two core words that rhyme.

9. _____   10. _____

CHALLENGE WORDS

Write the missing challenge words.

Jane loves every __(1)__ of animal.
She often __(2)__ to the woods with her
mother. Jane tries to __(3)__ animal
tracks. If she finds __(4)__ tracks, she
follows them. Jane moves quietly so
animals don't run __(5)__.

1. _____   2. _____   3. _____

4. _____   5. _____

PRACTICE

Write the missing core words.

Is someone in __(1)__ family a runner? Are you? These days, __(2)__ people in America are runners. It doesn't matter if they __(3)__ in the city or in the country. They run almost __(4)__ day.

Sometimes they run in a big race. It is a __(5)__ long race. All the runners are people __(6)__ can run far. They have to __(7)__ their very best before the race is over. Each runner __(8)__ have to go over 26 miles to reach the finish line.

9. One _____ I love to do is run a race!

10. Hey, _____ you running today?

1. _____
2. _____
3. _____
4. _____
5. _____
6. _____
7. _____
8. _____
9. _____
10. _____

WRITE WORD FAMILIES

Add the letters *ing* to make words.
Ring the word that names the picture.

1. s _____
2. br _____
3. r _____
4. k _____
5. st _____

92

DICTIONARY WORKOUT

At the top of each dictionary page are two words that help you find the page you are looking for. They are called guide words. Guide words tell you the first and last words on that page. Look at these guide words. Write the core words that belong on the same dictionary page as these guide words.

van / when   ← **guide words**

1. _____   2. _____

CORE WORDS

does

were

every

very

give

live

thing

your

many

who

WRITE RIGHT

Remember to round your circle letters so they will be easy to read. Practice writing each circle letter once.

abcdegopq

WRITE ON YOUR OWN

This runner is tired. He needs your help. Write some words to cheer him on. You may make your words rhyme if you want to.

UNIT **19**

Remember the beginning sound in *shoe* and the beginning sound in *when*. Find the missing letters. Then write the words.

what
shine
flash
why
clash
shore

1. fla___ _____

2. ___ine _____

3. ___y _____

4. ___at _____

5. cla___ _____

6. ___ore _____

FOCUS Ring in each word the letters that spell the beginning sound in *shoe* or *when*.

UNIT **20**

Remember the beginning sound in *child* and the beginning sound in *think*. Write the list word that rhymes with each word.

bath
teach
chick
thin
tooth
thank

1. truth _____

2. path _____

3. peach _____

4. sick _____

5. sank _____

6. tin _____

FOCUS Ring in each word the letters that spell the beginning sound in *child* or *think*.

UNIT 21

dark
art
cart
hard
park
yard

Remember the /är/ as in *farm*.
Write the word pairs that rhyme with
each picture word.

1. _____ 2. _____

3. _____ 4. _____

5. _____ 6. _____

FOCUS   Ring in each word the letters that spell /är/.

UNIT 22

first
horn
horse
shirt
for
short

Remember the /ėr/ as in *third* and the
sounds of *or* as in *more*.
Write the two words that have the same
middle sounds as the picture word.

1. _____ 2. _____

Write the word that rhymes with *or*.

3. _____

Write the three words whose middle
sounds are the same as *or*.

4. _____ 5. _____ 6. _____

FOCUS   Ring in each word the letters that
spell /ėr/ or the sounds of *or*.

95

give
who
every
were
does
thing

Remember that some words are not spelled as they sound. Find the missing letters in each word. Then write the words.

1. d___s _____

2. g__v__ _____

3. ev__ry _____

4. w__r__ _____

5. ___ing _____

6. ___o _____

FOCUS

Ring two words that you find hard to spell.

WRITE WORD FAMILIES

Use the first letter given in the writing lines. Write a word that rhymes with the word beside the number.

1. tooth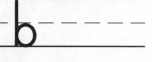

2. cart

3. horn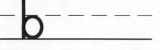

4. give

Add the ending *ing* to each word.

5. flash _____

6. teach _____

96

DICTIONARY WORKOUT

Below is part of a dictionary page.
Write the answers to the questions.

cart (kärt) **1** a vehicle with two wheels, used for carrying. **2** carry in a cart.

chick (chik) **1** a young chicken. **2** a young bird. **3** child.

clash (klash) **1** a loud hard sound. **2** a quarrel or disagreement.

How many entry words are given? 1. _____

How many definitions are there for *chick?* 2. _____

PROOFREAD

Write the punctuation mark that belongs at the end of each sentence.
Use these: . ! ?

1. Did you see that flash of light ○
2. Oh no, the light went out ○
3. We'll light a candle ○

1. ◯ 2. ◯ 3. ◯

1. _____

2. _____

3. _____

4. _____

5. _____

6. _____

7. _____

8. _____

9. _____

10. _____

1. brag
2. broom
3. brick
4. bright
5. frog
6. free
7. frisky
8. trade
9. train
10. trick

25 TRAIN A FROG

FOCUS

Say *bright*, *frog*, and *train*.
Listen to the beginning sounds.
Write the words.

1. _____

2. _____

3. _____

Ring the two letters that spell the beginning sounds in each word.

front   tramp
friend   treat
bread

98

LEARN Write a core word that rhymes with each word below.

Use core words that begin with *br*.

1. room

_____

_____

2. night

_____

_____

3. tag

_____

_____

4. sick

_____

_____

Use core words that begin with *fr*.

5. me

_____

_____

6. risky

_____

_____

7. log

_____

_____

Use core words that begin with *tr*.

8. chain

_____

_____

9. grade

_____

_____

10. chick

_____

_____

CHALLENGE WORDS

Write the missing challenge words. Ring the two letters that spell the beginning sounds in each word.

My dog Rags can act like a __(1)__ without a home. Rags goes to my friend's __(2)__ door. He barks for my __(3)__ to come out and give him a __(4)__ to eat. Rags will even eat __(5)__ !

1. _____

_____

2. _____

_____

3. _____

4. _____

5. _____

PRACTICE

Write the missing core words.

   Do you mind if I ___(1)___ a bit about my pet? My ___(2)___ is a wonderful pet. Its color is ___(3)___ green. It is very smart and also very ___(4)___. I can ___(5)___ my frog to do tricks. One ___(6)___ it learned is how to jump through a hoop. I wouldn't ___(7)___ my frog for anything. No, not ever!

Write the missing core word in each sentence.

The Third Little Pig made a ___(8)___ house.

Story books are ___(9)___ at the library.

In some tales, a witch rides on a ___(10)___.

1.	2.
3.	4.
5.	6.
7.	8.
9.	10.

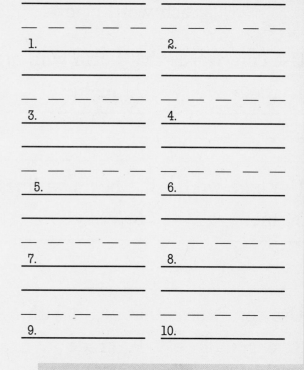

WRITE WORD FAMILIES

Add the letters *ain* to make words.
Ring the word that names the picture.

1. r   2. p   3. br

Add the letters *ag* to make words.

4. s   5. dr   6. b

100

COMMUNICATE

PROOFREAD

Remember to put a period after Mr.,
Mrs., and Ms.
Write this sentence. Put periods
where they belong.

Mr and Mrs Lee live there

WRITE RIGHT

Make all parts of your letter the right size so they will be
easy to read.

not clear

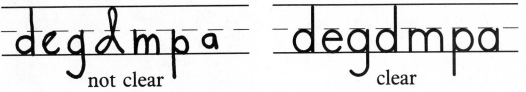
clear

Write these animal names: kitten turtle pony fish

WRITE ON YOUR OWN

This frog is magic! He will give you
three wishes. Write about three
things you might wish for.

CORE WORDS

brag
broom
brick
bright
frog
free
frisky
trade
train
trick

CORE

1. _____
2. _____
3. _____
4. _____
5. _____
6. _____
7. _____
8. _____
9. _____
10. _____

1. slam
2. sled
3. slip
4. slick
5. slide
6. space
7. speed
8. speech
9. spin
10. spy

FOCUS

Say *slide* and *spin*.
Listen to the beginning sounds
in each word.
Write *slide* and *spin*.

1. _____   2. _____

Ring the two letters that spell
the beginning sounds in each
word.

CHALLENGE

spoon   sleet
spoke   slant
spark

102

LEARN

Write five core words with the same beginning sounds as the picture name.

1. _____   2. _____   3. _____

4. _____   5. _____

Write five core words with the same beginning sounds as the picture name.

6. _____   7. _____   8. _____

9. _____   10. _____

CHALLENGE WORDS

Write the challenge words that begin like the picture name.

(2 words)

1. _____   2. _____

(3 words)

3. _____   4. _____

5. _____

PRACTICE

Write the missing core words.

    I pull my __(1)__ to the top of a hill. Then I get on the sled and __(2)__ down. I pick up __(3)__ going down. It feels as if I'm flying through __(4)__!

    I like to skate, too, on ice that is smooth and __(5)__. Sometimes I __(6)__ and fall. Other times I __(7)__ around like a top! Oh, I love winter!

1. _____ 2. _____

3. _____ 4. _____

5. _____ 6. _____

7. _____ 8. _____

9. _____ 10. _____

Write the missing core word for each sign.

Don't __(8)__ this door!

WANTED: a secret __(9)__

Quiet! A __(10)__ is being given!

WRITE WORD FAMILIES   Add the letters *eed* to make words.

1. f_____ 2. r_____ 3. W_____

4. b_____ 5. n_____

Ring the word that names the picture.

COMMUNICATE
PROOFREAD

A contraction is a short way of writing two words as one word. Use an apostrophe (') in a contraction to show where a letter or letters have been left out.

Write each contraction correctly with the apostrophe in place.

1. does not
   doesnt
   _____
   _ _ _ _ _ _ _

2. I am
   Im
   _____
   _ _ _ _ _ _ _

3. they will
   theyll
   _____
   _ _ _ _ _ _ _

4. can not
   cant
   _____
   _ _ _ _ _ _ _

CORE WORDS

slam
sled
slip
slick
slide
space
speed
speech
spin
spy

WRITE RIGHT

Close your circle letters to make them clear.

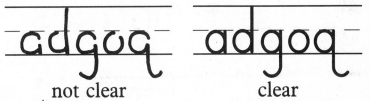

not clear   clear

Write these words. a quiet dog
_____
_ _ _ _ _ _ _ _ _ _ _ _ _ _ _ _
_____

WRITE ON YOUR OWN

Write about what you like to do best in winter. Proofread your writing.

105

1. _____

2. _____

3. _____

4. _____

5. _____

6. _____

7. _____

8. _____

9. _____

10. _____

1. animals
2. ants
3. chickens
4. seals
5. cows
6. ducks
7. rabbits
8. snakes
9. whales
10. zebras

27 MORE THAN ONE

FOCUS

You can add the letter *s* to many words to make them mean more than one. Words that name more than one are called plurals. Write the core word that tells about all the other words.

_____

_____

CHALLENGE

bears   chipmunks
lions   kangaroos
tigers

106

LEARN

Plural words name more than one.

Add the letter *s* to make the words plural.

1. one zebra,
   many ____ _____

2. one rabbit,
   a lot of ____ _____

3. one ant,
   many ____ _____

4. one chicken,
   two ____ _____

5. one cow,
   many ____ _____

6. one snake,
   four ____ _____

7. one whale,
   six ____ _____

8. one seal,
   a family of ____ _____

9. one duck,
   many ____ _____

10. one animal,
    many ____ _____

CHALLENGE WORDS

Write the challenge words that name the animals.

Ring the letter that makes each word plural.

1. They are large, have fur, and like
   to sleep during the winter.

2. They are large cats with stripes.

3. They are very large cats. The males have
   long hair around their faces.

4. They are very small animals with
   stripes down their backs.

5. The mothers carry their babies in
   pockets.

1. _____

2. _____

3. _____   4. _____   5. _____

107

PRACTICE

Write the core word that names each picture.

1. _____

2. _____

3. _____

4. _____

5. _____

6. _____

7. _____

8. _____

9. _____

10. What are all these living things called? _____

WRITE WORD FAMILIES

Make each word name "only one" by taking off the *s*. Write the new words.

1. chickens

   _____

2. ants

   _____

3. zebras

   _____

4. seals

   _____

5. whales

   _____

6. cows

   _____

COMMUNICATE
DICTIONARY WORKOUT

What if you wanted to look up the meaning of *ducks* in the dictionary?

You will not find *ducks* as an entry word.

You need to look up the word *duck*.

Many words have these endings: *s*, *es*, *ed*, *ing*.

If a word has an ending, look up the word without the ending.

What words would you look up in the dictionary to find the meanings of these words?

(Remember to take away the endings.)

1. chickens   2. animals   3. goes
4. marched   5. parking   6. farmed

1. _____
2. _____
3. _____
4. _____
5. _____
6. _____

WRITE RIGHT

Practice writing the letter *s* in the word *snakes*.

ssss

snakes _____ _____

WRITE ON YOUR OWN

Choose an animal for your pet. Give it a name. Write how you will keep the animal safe and happy.

Remember to proofread your writing.

1. _____
2. _____
3. _____
4. _____
5. _____
6. _____
7. _____
8. _____
9. _____
10. _____

1. see
2. sea
3. dear
4. deer
5. die
6. dye
7. meet
8. meat
9. road
10. rode

28
WE RODE THE BIG ROAD

FOCUS

Some words sound the same, but they have different spellings and different meanings. These words are called *homophones*. You have to remember the different spellings and different meanings of homophones.

Say *road* and *rode*.

These words are homophones.

Write the words *road* and *rode*.

_____   _____

1. _____   2. _____

Ring the letters that spell the long *o* sound in each word.

CHALLENGE

seam   too
seem   to
eye

110

LEARN

Write the pair of homophones that fits in each puzzle.

They should rhyme with the word beside the puzzle.

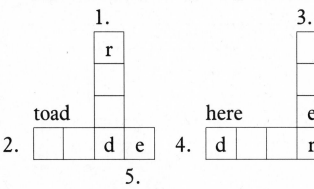
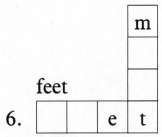
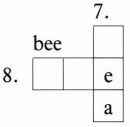
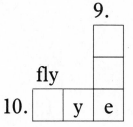

1. _____ 2. _____

3. _____ 4. _____

5. _____ 6. _____

7. _____ 8. _____

9. _____ 10. _____

CHALLENGE WORDS

Write the challenge words that fit in the sentences. They should also rhyme with the word at the beginning of each sentence.

1. _____ 2. _____

3. _____ 4. _____

5. _____

(dream) The elves __(1)__ to sew a __(2)__ without looking.

(pie) I can't see the __(3)__ of the needle.

(who) I would like __(4)__ sew that well __(5)__ !

111

PRACTICE

Write the missing core words.

Last summer, I went to see my __(1)__ grandfather. I __(2)__ on the bus. I looked out of the window and could __(3)__ many things. I saw a __(4)__ running. I saw people swimming in the __(5)__. I saw a man eating a __(6)__ sandwich in a car. All the time, the bus kept going down the __(7)__. At last we were there. I could __(8)__ my grandfather with a big hug!

Write the homophone that fits each sentence.

9. A fish out of water will ____.

10. Ned will ____ the shirt blue.

1. _____   2. _____

3. _____   4. _____

5. _____   6. _____

7. _____   8. _____

9. _____   10. _____

WRITE WORD FAMILIES

Make the words mean more than one. Add the ending *s*. Write each word.

1. sea   2. meat   3. road

_____   _____   _____

_____   _____   _____

Add the ending *ing* to each word. Write the word where it belongs in the sentence.

4. see + ing   5. meet + ing

_____   _____

I liked _____ you and _____ your family.

112

COMMUNICATE
PROOFREAD

CORE WORDS

Homophones are words that sound alike but have different spellings and meanings. Find the word in each sentence that is not used correctly. Then write the homophone for that word.

see

sea

dear

deer

1. The Indian boy road on a horse.

die

dye

meat

2. Did he meat anything along the way?

meet

road

3. He almost met a running dear.

rode

4. He could sea the white on its tail.

1. _____

2. _____

3. _____

4. _____

WRITE RIGHT

Remember to close the letters *o* and *a* so they will be easy to read.

c a

not clear

o a

clear

Write: The toad sat on the road.

_____

WRITE ON YOUR OWN

You are away on a trip. Write to a friend and tell how you got there. Write about the best day and what you did. Be sure to close the letters *o* and *a* as you write them.

29

MY FAMILY

1. _____
2. _____
3. _____
4. _____
5. _____
6. _____
7. _____
8. _____
9. _____
10. _____

1. family
2. mother
3. father
4. sister
5. brother
6. grandmother
7. grandfather
8. aunt
9. uncle
10. baby

FOCUS

You will use words that tell about your family often in your writing. These family words have many sounds you have learned to spell.

Write the core word that tells about all the other words.

_____

_____

CHALLENGE

parent   children
person   together
twins

LEARN

Write the missing core words.

This is Tim's __(1)__ tree. Sue and Dan are his __(2)__ and __(3)__. Sam is his __(4)__ brother. Ann and Tom are his __(5)__ and __(6)__. Ann's brother Ted and sister Em are Tim's __(7)__ and __(8)__. Ann's mother and father are Tim's __(9)__ and __(10)__.

1. _____
2. _____
3. _____
4. _____

5. _____
6. _____
7. _____
8. _____

9. _____
10. _____

CHALLENGE WORDS

Write the missing challenge words.

1. Tim's mother or father is his ____.
2. Tim and Dan are ____.
3. Tim, Dan, Sue, and Sam are all ____.
4. Tim's family likes to play ____.
5. Tim loves every ____ in his family.

1. _____
2. _____
3. _____

4. _____
5. _____

PRACTICE

Write the missing core words.

Mom is the name I call my __(1)__.
I call my __(2)__ Dad. Grandma is
the name I call my __(3)__. And
Grandpa is how I call my __(4)__. I
call my __(5)__ Sis. And sometimes
I call my __(6)__ brother Pal.

Write the word that goes with
each clue.

7. your mother's brother
8. your father's sister
9. one of two boys in a family
10. mother, father, and their
    children

1. _____ 2. _____

3. _____

4. _____

5. _____ 6. _____

7. _____ 8. _____

9. _____ 10. _____

WRITE WORD FAMILIES

Make each word mean more than one.
Use the letter *s* at the end of each word.

1. grandfather
_____

2. grandmother
_____

3. mother
_____

4. aunt
_____

5. brother
_____

6. fathers
_____

COMMUNICATE

DICTIONARY WORKOUT

What words would you look up in the dictionary to find the meanings of these words? (Remember to take away the endings.)

1. sisters

_____
_ _ _ _ _ _ _
_____

2. uncles

_____
_ _ _ _ _ _ _
_____

3. walking

_____
_ _ _ _ _ _ _
_____

4. asked

_____
_ _ _ _ _ _ _
_____

5. boxes

_____
_ _ _ _ _ _ _
_____

6. spelling

_____
_ _ _ _ _ _ _
_____

WRITE RIGHT

Do not press down too lightly or too hard.

too hard   too light   clear

Write this sentence.   This is my family.

_____
_ _
_____

WRITE ON YOUR OWN

Write about a special person. It can be someone in your family. Tell why you think that person is special.

117

UNIT 25

brag
brick
trade
train
frisky
trick

Remember the beginning sounds in
bread, *friend*, and *trip*.
Write two core words that begin like
each word.

bread   1. _____   2. _____

friend   3. _____   4. _____

trip   5. _____   6. _____

FOCUS   Ring in each word the two letters that
spell the beginning sounds.

UNIT 26

speech
slide
spy
slick
slip
speed

Remember the beginning sounds in *sleep* and *spell*.
Find the missing letters. Then write the words.

1. ___ick _____   2. ___ip _____

3. ___ide _____   4. ___y _____

5. ___eech _____   6. ___eed _____

FOCUS   Ring in each word the two letters that
spell the beginning sounds.

UNIT 27

Remember to add *s* to make some words mean more than one. Make these words mean more than one.

chickens
snakes
seals
ants
rabbits
whales

ant   1. _____   rabbit   2. _____

chicken   3. _____   seal   4. _____

snake   5. _____   whale   6. _____

FOCUS

Ring in each word the letter that makes the word mean more than one.

UNIT 28

Remember homophones such as *to* and *two*. Name the picture words. Then write the two homophones that rhyme with each one.

meat
road
rode
die
meet
dye

1. _____   2. _____

3. _____   4. _____

5. _____   6. _____

FOCUS

Ring the pairs of words that are homophones.

Remember family words such as *mother* and *father*.

Write the word that goes with each clue.

sister
family
aunt
brother
grandmother
uncle

1. mom's sister _____

2. boy child _____

3. dad's brother _____

4. girl child _____

5. dad's mother _____

6. all of you _____

FOCUS

Ring the word that tells what all the other words are about.

WRITE WORD FAMILIES

Do the Word Math. Write the new words.

1. train − tr + r = _____

2. slide − sl + h = _____

3. p + ants = _____

4. meet − m + f = _____

Remember that adding the ending *s* makes a word mean more than one.

Write these words so they mean more than one.

5. meat _____

6. brother _____

DICTIONARY WORKOUT

What words would you look up in the
dictionary to find the meanings of
these words? Write the words.
(Remember to take away the endings.)

1. fathers _____
   _____

2. trained _____
   _____

3. speeding _____
   _____

PROOFREAD

An *apostrophe* is used to show who owns
something. Write each dark word with an
apostrophe where it belongs.

1. This is **Marys** bird.
   _____
   This is _____ bird.

2. These are **Bens** rabbits.
   _____
   These are _____ rabbits.

An apostrophe is used in contractions
(*didn't, can't*). Write each dark word
with an apostrophe where it belongs.

3. **Whats** in the box?
   _____
   _____

4. **Its** a ball.
   _____
   _____

CORE

1. _____
2. _____
3. _____
4. _____
5. _____
6. _____
7. _____
8. _____
9. _____
10. _____

1. bush
2. push
3. pull
4. full
5. foot
6. book
7. hook
8. took
9. wool
10. good

FOCUS

Say *push* and *book*.
Listen to the middle sound in
each word.
The sign for this sound is /u̇/.
The letters *oo* and *u* can be used
to spell /u̇/.
Write *push* and *book*.

_____   _____

1. _____   2. _____

Ring the letter or letters that
spell /u̇/ in each word.

CHALLENGE

brook   cookbook
crook   stood
shook

LEARN

Use core words in which /u̇/ is spelled *u*.
Write two rhyming pairs of words. (4 words)

‗‗‗‗‗‗‗‗‗‗   ‗‗‗‗‗‗‗‗‗‗   ‗‗‗‗‗‗‗‗‗‗   ‗‗‗‗‗‗‗‗‗‗

1. ‗‗‗‗‗‗‗   2. ‗‗‗‗‗‗‗   3. ‗‗‗‗‗‗‗   4. ‗‗‗‗‗‗‗

Use core words in which /u̇/ is spelled *oo*.
Write three words that rhyme with one another.

‗‗‗‗‗‗‗‗‗‗   ‗‗‗‗‗‗‗‗‗‗   ‗‗‗‗‗‗‗‗‗‗

5. ‗‗‗‗‗‗‗   6. ‗‗‗‗‗‗‗   7. ‗‗‗‗‗‗‗

Write the core words that begin with
the same sound as the picture names.

‗‗‗‗‗‗‗‗‗‗   ‗‗‗‗‗‗‗‗‗‗   ‗‗‗‗‗‗‗‗‗‗

8. ‗‗‗‗‗‗‗   9. ‗‗‗‗‗‗‗   10. ‗‗‗‗‗‗‗

CHALLENGE WORDS

Write the challenge word that fits
each clue.

1. This book tells how to cook.

2. This is a little stream.

3. This is what the wind did to the
   trees.

4. This is what people did when they
   got up to leave.

5. This word rhymes with *hook*. It
   also means hook.

6. These letters spell /u̇/ in all the
   challenge words.

‗‗‗‗‗‗‗‗‗‗   ‗‗‗‗‗‗‗‗‗‗
1. ‗‗‗‗‗‗‗   2. ‗‗‗‗‗‗‗

‗‗‗‗‗‗‗‗‗‗   ‗‗‗‗‗‗‗‗‗‗
3. ‗‗‗‗‗‗‗   4. ‗‗‗‗‗‗‗

‗‗‗‗‗‗‗‗‗‗   ‗‗‗‗‗‗‗‗‗‗
5. ‗‗‗‗‗‗‗   6. ‗‗‗‗‗‗‗

PRACTICE Write the missing core words.

Pull and Push

How Not to Fish

Funny Fred

The first book tells you how to row a boat. It tells how to __(1)__ toward yourself and __(2)__ away from yourself to row a boat. The boy in the picture has his fishing __(3)__ caught in a __(4)__ ! His pail is __(5)__ of fish.

The third __(6)__ is a __(7)__ one. I __(8)__ it out of the library. It's about a boy who wears one red __(9)__ sock. On the other __(10)__ he wears a yellow sock. He does this so he can tell his feet apart.

1. _____   2. _____

3. _____   4. _____

5. _____   6. _____

7. _____   8. _____

9. _____   10. _____

WRITE WORD FAMILIES

Add the ending *ing* to tell about the present.

1. pull

_____

I am _____ it.

2. push

_____

I am _____ it.

Add the ending *ed* to tell about the past.

3. pull

_____

I _____ it.

4. hook

_____

I _____ it.

5. push

_____

I _____ it.

124

COMMUNICATE
DICTIONARY WORKOUT

f@mily f◎ot f☺ll

The three words above are in ABC order.
When the first letters are the same, put
words in ABC order by the second letters.
Write each set of words in ABC order.

bush
book _____ _____ _____
brick 1._____ 2._____ 3._____

took
twins _____ _____ _____
task 4._____ 5._____ 6._____

WRITE RIGHT   Leave the right space between letters in words.

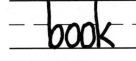 

not clear   not clear   clear

Write this sentence.   Who took the book?

_____

_____

WRITE ON YOUR OWN

Write about a book you liked. Give
the name of the book and tell what it
was about. Remember to leave spaces
between letters.

125

CORE

1. _____
2. _____
3. _____
4. _____
5. _____
6. _____
7. _____
8. _____
9. _____
10. _____

1. bat
2. batting
3. cut
4. cutting
5. hit
6. hitting
7. mop
8. mopped
9. tap
10. tapped

CHALLENGE

running   digging
skipping   begged
hopping

FOCUS

Look at these words:

        bat   tap

How many syllables does
each word have? _____

1. _____

How many letters spell the
vowel sound? _____

2. _____

How many letters spell the
last consonant _____
sound?

3. _____

Look at these words:
batting, tapped. What was
done to *bat* and *tap* when
ing or *ed* was added?

_____

4. _____

LEARN

Write three core words with the same
ending sound as the picture name.

1. _____ 2. _____ 3. _____

Write three core words that end in *ing*.
Remember:

_ _ _ t + t + ing

4. _____ 5. _____ 6. _____

Write two core words with the same
ending sound as the picture name.

7. _____ 8. _____

Write two core words that end in *ed*.
Remember:

_ _ p + p + ed

9. _____ 10. _____

CHALLENGE WORDS

Write the missing challenge words.

They forgot about lunch. Dan was
(1) a hole. Rita was (2) a race.
Sandy was (3) rope. Hal was (4)
on one foot. Only our dog (5) for
something to eat.

1. _____

2. _____

3. _____ 4. _____ 5. _____

Ring the double letters in each word.

127

PRACTICE

Write the missing core words.

    Our baseball game was tied, five to five. The coach said, "Who's up to __(1)__ now?"

    Kim __(2)__ me on the shoulder. "You're __(3)__ now," she said.

    "Oh no!" I thought. "I'm not very good at __(4)__ the ball. Maybe I'm not __(5)__ out to play ball at all."

    But my friends cheered me on. I __(6)__ a home run!

Write the words that complete the sentences. The words should rhyme with the underlined words.

7. I stopped reading and __(7)__ the floor.
8. Lilly wears a red cap when she __(8)__ dances.
9. I'll start __(9)__ the grass while you are shutting in the dog.
10. I'll __(10)__ the floor when I stop.

1. _____
2. _____
3. _____
4. _____
5. _____
6. _____
7. _____
8. _____
9. _____
10. _____

WRITE WORD FAMILIES   Write the words and add the ending *ing*.

1. rub + b + ing _____
2. tug + g + ing _____

Write the words and add the ending *ed*.

3. grin + n + ed _____
4. trim + m + ed _____

COMMUNICATE

PROOFREAD

Notice how you should use a comma in dates.

    July 4, 1776   August 23, 1989

Write all the dates you see in this
baseball calendar. Put commas where
they belong.

    Opening game: May 14 1989

    Fireworks game: July 4 1989

    Last game: October 15 1989

1. _____   2. _____

3. _____

WRITE RIGHT   Leave the right space between letters.

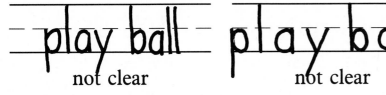

play ball   play ball   play ball

    not clear   not clear   clear

Write this sentence.   The team is hitting today!

WRITE ON YOUR OWN

Look at the girl running to home
plate. Write about how she feels.
Remember to proofread your writing.

129

33
NOW—A CIRCUS CLOWN

CORE

1. _____
2. _____
3. _____
4. _____
5. _____
6. _____
7. _____
8. _____
9. _____
10. _____

1. now
2. owl
3. down
4. town
5. clown
6. out
7. loud
8. sound
9. house
10. ouch

FOCUS

Say *clown* and *loud*.
Listen to the middle sound in each word.
The dictionary sign for this sound is /ou/.
The letters *ow* and *ou* spell /ou/ in these words.
Write *clown* and *loud*.

1. _____ 2. _____

Ring the two letters that spell /ou/ in each word.

CHALLENGE

found   howl
around   crown
south

130

LEARN

Use words in which /ou/ is spelled *ou*.
Write five core words with the same
ending sounds as the picture names.

1. _____

2. _____

3. _____

4. _____

5. _____

Use words in which /ou/ is spelled *ow*.
Write two core words that rhyme
with the picture names.

6. _____

7. _____

Write three core words that rhyme.

8. _____

9. _____

10. _____

CHALLENGE WORDS

Write a challenge word for each clue.

1. the sound a wolf makes
2. what a king wears on his head
3. not north, east, or west
4. the way a merry-go-round goes
5. not lost anymore

1. _____

2. _____

3. _____

4. _____

5. _____

Ring the letters that spell /ou/ in each word.

PRACTICE

Write the missing core words.

I love it when the circus comes to __(1)__ ! It is here right __(2)__ . Last night, my family went to see it. We heard the __(3)__ shouts of the people selling popcorn. We heard a banging __(4)__ when a person was shot out of a big gun! He came __(5)__ in a net. We saw a funny __(6)__ . He fell off a couch and said __(7)__ !

It was late at night when we came __(8)__ of the circus. I still didn't want to go back to our __(9)__ . Mom said I was a night __(10)__ !

1. _____ 2. _____

3. _____ 4. _____

5. _____ 6. _____

7. _____ 8. _____

9. _____ 10. _____

WRITE WORD FAMILIES

Do this Word Math. Make more words.

sound − s + b = _____

sound − s + p = _____

sound − s + gr = _____

1. _____

2. _____

3. _____

loud − l + cl = _____

loud − l + pr = _____

4. _____

5. _____

COMMUNICATE

DICTIONARY WORKOUT

Write each group of words in ABC order.
Remember to look at the second letters.

CORE WORDS

now
owl
down
town
clown
out
loud
sound
house
ouch

1. owl, out, down

_____ _____ _____
_ _ _ _ _ _ _ _ _ _ _ _ _ _ _
_____ _____ _____

2. now, sound, nut

_____ _____ _____
_ _ _ _ _ _ _ _ _ _ _ _ _ _ _
_____ _____ _____

WRITE RIGHT   Capital letters touch the top line.
Use capital letters to write this sign.

MY MOUSE IS NAPPING.
NO LOUD SOUNDS, PLEASE!

_____
_ _
_____
_ _
_____
_ _
_____

WRITE ON YOUR OWN

Look at Bumble the Clown! Tell what she is doing. Begin your story with a sentence that begins like this: *Bumble is a silly clown because . . . .* Remember to proofread your writing.

133

1. _____
2. _____
3. _____
4. _____
5. _____
6. _____
7. _____
8. _____
9. _____
10. _____

1. firepole
2. bedroom
3. lunchbox
4. notebook
5. doghouse
6. something
7. catfish
8. football
9. into
10. inside

FOCUS

A compound word is two words put together to make one word. The spelling words on this page are all compound words. One of those words is *inside*.
Say *inside*. Write the word.

_____

_____

Ring the two words that were put together to make the compound word.

CHALLENGE

downtown   weekend

sailboat   everywhere

sandbox

134

LEARN

Find a word in Box B that goes with a numbered word in Box A to make a compound word. Write the core words.

Box A

1.	lunch	6.	bed
2.	in	7.	in
3.	note	8.	dog
4.	foot	9.	some
5.	cat	10.	fire

Box B

pole	house
ball	room
thing	box
to	book
fish	side

1. _____

2. _____

3. _____

4. _____

5. _____

6. _____

7. _____

8. _____

9. _____

10. _____

CHALLENGE WORDS

Write the missing challenge words.

Last __(1)__ was busy for Max. He went __(2)__ to shop. He played in the __(3)__ at the park. He watched a __(4)__ on the lake. Max had fun __(5)__ he went!

1. _____

2. _____

3. _____

4. _____

5. _____

PRACTICE

Write the missing core words.

Mary brought her lunch to school in a __(1)__ . She wondered what was __(2)__ . What had her mother put __(3)__ the lunchbox?

Mary found __(4)__ she loved to eat. It was cooked, cold __(5)__ !

Write a core word to answer each question.

6. What do firefighters slide down?
7. What can you write notes in?
8. What kind of ball do you kick?
9. What room is for sleeping?
10. What house is for a dog?

1. _____
2. _____
3. _____
4. _____
5. _____
6. _____
7. _____
8. _____
9. _____
10. _____

WRITE WORD FAMILIES

Make compound words. Put the words together and write the new word.

any + thing

1. _____

barn + yard

2. _____

sea + shore

3. _____

club + house

4. _____

some + where

5. _____

space + ship

6. _____

136

COMMUNICATE
PROOFREAD

Look at the *comma* in each address:

city   **state**   **city**   **state**

Albany, New York   Houston, Texas

A comma is used to separate the name
of a city from the name of its state.
Write the make-believe addresses below.
Put commas where they belong.

city   **state**

Catfish   California

Lunchbox   Louisiana

1. _____   2. _____

WRITE RIGHT

Make sure your small letters touch
the middle line.

Write this sentence.   Our classroom was busy.

WRITE ON YOUR OWN

Your lunch is packed inside this
lunchbox. Tell what you would like
to find inside. Use words that tell
how good the food would be.

1. _____
2. _____
3. _____
4. _____
5. _____
6. _____
7. _____
8. _____
9. _____
10. _____

1. one
2. two
3. three
4. four
5. five
6. six
7. seven
8. eight
9. nine
10. ten

35
ONE, TWO, THREE!

FOCUS

These words help you write about numbers.

    one   two   eight

Look at the letters that spell each word.

Write the word that is a homophone for each word below.

    won   too   ate

1. _____
2. _____
3. _____

CHALLENGE

add   count

minus   numbers

second

138

LEARN

Write the core words that tell how many are in each picture.

1. _____

2. _____

3. _____

4. _____

5. _____

6. _____

7. _____

8. _____

9. _____

10. _____

CHALLENGE WORDS

Write the challenge word that fits in each sentence.

1. Can you _____ from 1 to 100?
2. *One, two, three,* and *four* are _____.
3. If you _____ 2 and 2, you get 4.
4. Three _____ one is two.
5. Between *first* and *third* is _____.

1. _____

2. _____

3. _____

4. _____

5. _____

139

PRACTICE

Write the core word that answers each question.

1. How many fingers are on one hand?
2. How many toes are on both feet?
3. How many ears does a dog have?
4. How many lines are in this shape? △
5. How many people are in two pairs of twins?
6. How many noses are on one face?
7. How many legs does an insect have?
8. What number comes after eight?
9. What is two less than ten?
10. How many days are in one week?

1. _____   2. _____

3. _____   4. _____

5. _____   6. _____

7. _____   8. _____

9. _____   10. _____

WRITE WORD FAMILIES

Write the core words and add new endings.
Add the letter *s*.

2 + s	3 + s	5 + s
1. _____	2. _____	3. _____

Add *teen*.

4 + teen	9 + teen	6 + teen
4. _____	5. _____	6. _____

COMMUNICATE

DICTIONARY WORKOUT

Write the answer to each question.
Use the dictionary entry.

one two three four five six seven eight nine ten

> **one** (wun) **1** the number 1. **2** a single person or thing. *Pick the one you like best.* **3** a person who stands for people in general. *One must try hard.*

1. What is the entry word? _____

2. How many meanings does it have? _____

3. Would the word *open* come before or after this word in the dictionary? _____

WRITE RIGHT   Make your numerals easy to read.

1 2 3 4 5 6 7 8 9 10

Write the numerals from 1 to 10.

_____

_____

WRITE ON YOUR OWN

What number do you want on the back of your shirt? Write about the number you like best. Tell why you like it.

Remember the /u̇/ as in *foot*.
Write the groups of words that rhyme.

book

hook

full

took

pull

wool

1. _____ 2. _____ 3. _____

4. _____ 5. _____ 6. _____

FOCUS Ring in each word the letter or letters
that spell /u̇/.

Remember that for some words you
double the last letter before you add
ing or *ed* (*bat*, *batting*). Write the
word pairs that have the same
beginning sound as each picture name.

mop

mopped

cut

cutting

hit

hitting

1. _____ 2. _____

3. _____ 4. _____

5. _____ 6. _____

FOCUS In the first word of each pair, ring the
letter that is doubled before the ending is
added.

UNIT 33

ouch
now
clown
out
owl
house

Remember the /ou/ as in *sound*.
Write the three words that have the
same beginning sound.

_____   _____   _____

1._____   2._____   3._____

Write the word that rhymes with each word below.

mouse   cow   town

_____   _____   _____

4._____   5._____   6._____

FOCUS

Ring the letters in each word that
spell /ou/.

UNIT 34

football
notebook
doghouse
bedroom
inside
lunchbox

Remember compound words such as
sandbox. Find the missing word. Then
write the compound words.

_____   _____

1. foot– _____   2. –house _____

_____   _____

3. –room _____   4. lunch– _____

_____   _____

5. –side _____   6. –book _____

FOCUS   Draw a line between the two words
that make each compound word.

Remember the number words such as *nine*.
Write the number word that fits each clue.

ten

seven

three

eight

five

four

1. before four _____

2. after seven _____

3. after six _____

4. before six _____

5. after three _____

6. after nine _____

FOCUS

Ring the number words for 3, 5, and 10.

WRITE WORD FAMILIES

Add the ending *ed* to each word.
Write the new words.

1. pull _____

2. hook _____

Add the ending *s* to each word.
Write the new words.

3. mop _____

4. clown _____

5. football _____

6. seven _____

DICTIONARY WORKOUT

Write the answer to each question.
Use the dictionary entry.

> **hit** (hit)   **1** give a blow;
> strike.   **2** a successful
> try.   **3** a hitting of the
> baseball by a batter.

_____
_ _ _ _ _ _ _

1. What is the entry word?   _____

_____
_ _ _ _ _ _ _

2. How many meanings does it have?   _____

_____
_ _ _ _ _ _ _

3. Would the word _hook_ come before
   or after this word in the dictionary?   _____

_____
_ _ _ _ _ _ _

4. What entry word would you look
   up to find the meaning of the word _hitting?_   _____

PROOFREAD

A comma is used in dates or in
addresses:

    October 20, 1980   New York, New York

Write this date and address. Put the
commas where they belong.

    May 14 1986   Bangor Maine
_____   _____
_ _ _ _ _ _ _   _ _ _ _ _ _ _
_____   _____

WHEN YOU WRITE

Read these ideas. They will help you make your stories and reports sparkle.

1. **Choose an idea.**

   Do you know enough about this idea?

   Will others be interested?

2. **Think about what you will write.**

3. **Write your first copy.**

   Don't worry about mistakes yet.

4. **Check your writing.**

   Look for spelling mistakes.

   Look for other mistakes.

   Do you like what you read?

   If not, make changes.

5. **Write the final copy.**

   Read your work again.

   Enjoy and share it if you like.

PROOFREADING CHECKLIST

Here are some things to look for when you are proofreading:

1. Did you start each sentence with a capital letter?

2. Did you end each sentence with the right punctuation mark?

3. Did you spell all the words correctly?

4. Did you capitalize all proper nouns?

5. Do you need to add or take out spaces?

HANDWRITING

Neat, clear handwriting is important.
It should be easy for people to read your written
work. Then they can understand it.
Take time to practice good
handwriting. Use these models for help.

Aa Bb Cc Dd Ee

Ff Gg Hh Ii Jj

Kk Ll Mm Nn

Oo Pp Qq Rr

Ss Tt Uu Vv

Ww Xx Yy Zz

POSSESSIVES

Possessives tell that something belongs to someone or something. Many possessives have an apostrophe. Follow these examples for making words possessive.

Possessives with singular nouns

Add an apostrophe (') and *s* to singular nouns.

a *dog's* collar   the *girl's* sneakers

Possessives with plural nouns

Add only an apostrophe (') to plural nouns that end in *s*.

the six *swans'* lake   most *boys'* teams

Add an apostrophe (') and *s* to plural nouns that do not end in *s*.

people's houses   many *mice's* tracks

ABBREVIATIONS

Abbreviations are short forms of certain words. Many abbreviations begin with a capital letter. Many end with a period. Read the abbreviations below. Notice which letters are left out of each abbreviation. Notice where the period is placed.

Sunday = Sun.   January = Jan.

Doctor = Dr.   Street = St.

CONTRACTIONS

Contractions join two words in a short form. An apostrophe shows where a letter or letters are left out. Read the contractions below. Notice which letters are left out. Notice where the apostrophe is placed.

it is = it's   we were = we're

can not = can't   I have = I've

WORDS OFTEN MISSPELLED

Some words are hard to spell. They may not look the way they sound. Or they may not follow spelling rules. The list below shows some of these words. Study the words in the list. Learn how to spell them.

again	for	my	trouble
always	friend	nothing	two
any	from	of	very
are	give	once	want
been	goes	said	was
children	guess	school	were
color	have	shoe	where
come	her	some	who
could	here	the	work
do	I	their	you
does	live	they	your
done	love	to	
every	many	too	

TAKING TESTS

This book contains different kinds of tests.

Follow these pointers to do well:

    1. Be sure you understand the directions.

    2. Read all the answers. Then make your choice.

    3. Fill in the answer circle carefully.

Read the test questions below. They will show you the different kinds of tests in this book.

Decide if the spelling of the underlined word is correct or incorrect. Fill in the circle beside your answer.

1. It was <u>badd</u> for the box to get wet.
    ⓐ correct   ● incorrect

2. There is no more <u>gas</u> in the bus.
    ● correct   ⓑ incorrect

Read the words in each group. Decide which word is spelled incorrectly. Fill in the answer circle that goes with that word.

1. ⓐ fix   2. ● tep
   ⓑ pink   ⓑ chin
   ● pinn   ⓒ if

SPELLING PRINCIPLES

1

Short *a* or /a/ may be spelled *a*.
man   hat

2

Short *i* or /i/ may be spelled *i*.
fix   mix

3

Short *o* or /o/ may be spelled *o*.
lot

The vowel sound /ô/ may be
spelled o.
dog

4

The ending sound /k/ may
be spelled *ck*.
pack   snack

5

Some words end with the
sounds of the letters *nd* or
st.
sand   just

7

Short *e* or /e/ may be spelled *e*.
fed   nest

8

Short *u* or /u/ may be spelled *u*.
rub   mud

9

Some words begin with the
sounds of the letters *dr, gr,*
or *tr*.
drive   grin   truck

10

Some words begin with the sounds of the letters *bl*, *gl*, or *pl*.

blast   **glad**   **plum**

11

Some words end with the sounds of the letters *sk*, *mp*, or *ng*.

mask   **camp**   **song**

13

Long *a* or /ā/ may be spelled *a-e*, *ai*, or *ay*.

came   **pail**   **hay**

14

Long *e* or /ē/ may be spelled *ea* or *ee*.

bean   **seen**

15

Long *i* or /ī/ may be spelled *i-e*, *y*, or *igh*.

pine   **fly**   **night**

16

Long *o* or /ō/ may be spelled *o-e*, *oa*, or *ow*.

poke   **goat**   **blow**

17

The vowel sound /ü/ may be spelled *u-e*, or *oo*.

tune   **200**

19

Some words begin with the sound of the letters *wh*.

why   **where**

Some words begin with the sound of *sh*. Some words end with the sound of *sh*.

shine   **clash**

20

Some words begin with the sound of *ch*. Some words end with the sound of *ch*.

chick   **teach**

Some words begin with the sound of *th*. Some words end with the sound of *th*.

thin   **tooth**

21

The vowel plus *r* sound /är/ may be spelled *ar*.

barn   **farm**

22

Many words have the sound of *or*.

horse

The vowel plus *r* sound /ėr/ may be spelled *ir*.

first

23

The English language has many words that do not follow the regular rules of spelling.

many   **who**

25

Many words begin with the sounds of the letters *br*, *fr*, or *tr*.

bright   **frog**   **train**

26

Many words begin with the sounds of the letters *sl* and *sp*.

slide   **spin**

27

The plural form of many words ends in *-s*

28

Words that sound the same but are spelled differently and have different meanings are called *homophones*.

road   **rode**

31

The vowel sound /u̇/ may be spelled *u* or *oo*.

push   **book**

32

Some one-syllable words have one-letter vowels and one final consonant. These words double the final consonant before an ending is added.

bat—batting

mop—mopping

33

The vowel sound /ou/ may be spelled *ow* or *ou*.

clown   **loud**

34

Compound words are formed by joining two other words.

lunchbox

HOW TO USE A DICTIONARY

A dictionary *entry* shows how to spell a
word. It also shows how to say and use the
word. Read this dictionary entry. Notice
all it shows about a word.

The *entry word* is the word
you look up. Entry words are
listed in alphabetical order.

The *respelling* tells how
to say the entry word.

What *part
of speech*
is the entry
word? The
abbreviation
says *n*.
This entry
word is a
noun.

bi cycle /bī′sik′el/ *n.* something with two wheels that a
person rides on. *He rode his
bicycle through the park.*

The *definition*
tells what the
entry word means.

This *sentence* shows how
to use the entry word.

Now you're ready to use the dictionary!

A

add /ad/ **1** to join numbers to get a sum. *If you add 3 and 5, you get 8.* **2** to say more. *Always add "please" when you ask for something.* **adds, added, adding.**

aid /ād/ **1** to help out. *Doctors aid the sick.* **aids, aided, aiding. 2** a help. *The woman asked for aid in pushing the car.*

a larm /ə larm´/ **1** a sudden fear of danger. *Alarm filled the girl when the dog broke loose.* **alarms. 2** to scare; to make someone afraid. *I think that seeing a snake would alarm me.* **3** a bell or sound that wakes people or tells of danger.

The alarm sounded when smoke from the fire filled the room. **alarms, alarmed, alarming.**

and /and/ or /ənd/ as well as. *Put on a coat and a hat.*

an i mal /an´ə məl/ a living thing that can eat, feel, and move about, such as a dog, cat, or snake. *A whale is a very large animal.* **animals.**

ant /ant/ one of the small bugs that live in the ground. *An ant has six tiny legs.* **ants.**

an y /en´ē/ **1** one thing or person out of many. *Sit in any chair you want.* **2** some. *Do you want any soup?*

a	hat
ā	age
ä	far
e	let
ē	equal
ėr	term
i	it
ī	ice
o	hot
ō	open
ô	order
oi	oil
ou	out
u	cup
ů	put
ü	rule
ch	child
ng	long
sh	she
th	thin
ͨH	then
zh	measure

ə = { a in about, e in taken, i in pencil, o in lemon, u in circus }

ant

arm /ärm/ part of the body between the hand and the shoulder. *She broke her arm when she fell.* **arms.**

a round /ə round´/ **1** in a circle. *She made the top spin around and around.* **2** on every side. *They planted flowers around the house.*

art

art /ärt/ drawings, paintings, and other works. *You can see great art in a museum.* **arts.**

as /az/ or /əz/ **1** equal to. *Jill sings as well as Jane.* **2** in the same way. *He cooked the meal as Mother would.*

ask /ask/ **1** to try to find an answer by words. *She will ask who the new boy is.* **2** to invite. *Will he ask me to his party?* **asks, asked, asking.**

aunt /ant/ **1** your father's or mother's sister. **2** your uncle's wife. *Aunt Rose will visit us soon.* **aunts.**

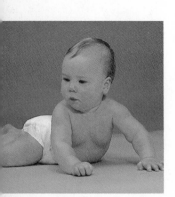

baby

a way /ə wā´/ **1** to a place apart. *She went away from home.* **2** not present; gone. *Our teacher is away today.*

B

ba by /bā´bē/ a child of a very young age. *Feed the baby a bottle of milk.* **babies.**

back pack /bak´pak´/ something worn on one's back and used for carrying things. *The child put her lunch in her backpack.* **backpacks.**

bad /bad/ **1** not the way it should be. *It is bad for your ears to play the TV too loudly.* **2** that which is wrong; evil. *The bad giant chased the queen.* **3** not pleasant, not nice. *Mother had a bad day at work.*

bait /bāt/ **1** food used to catch fish or other animals. *We use worms for bait when we fish.* **2** to put food on a hook or in a trap to catch an animal.

Can you help me bait my hook? **baits, baited, baiting.**

bal loon /ba lün′/ a bag filled with a gas to make it go up and float in the air. *The child's balloon floated away.* **balloons.**

band /band/ **1** a number of people joined together. *A band of hunters was looking for deer.* **2** a number of people joined together to play music. *Would you like to play drums for the school band?* **bands.**

barn /bärn/ a farm building used to keep animal food and to house cows and horses. *Our new barn is red.* **barns.**

bat /bat/ **1** a stick made of wood that is used to hit a baseball. **bats.** **2** to hit with a bat. *Who will bat next?* **bats, batted, batting.**

bath /bath/ the washing of the body. *After playing in the mud, the child needed a bath.* **baths.**

be /bē/ to act, exist. *I will be at home on Saturday.* **was** or **were, been, being.**

bean /bēn/ **a** smooth and fairly flat seed, used as a vegetable. *I ate the last bean on my plate.* **beans.**

bear /bear/ or /bar/ a large animal with thick fur and a short tail. *A bear likes to sleep in winter.* **bears.**

bed room /bed′rüm′/ a room in which people sleep. **bedrooms.**

beg /beg/ **1** to ask others to give something for nothing. *The mayor will beg for aid in his speech.* **begs, begged, begging.**

bend /bend/ **1** the part that turns or curves so that it is not straight. *Turn sharply at the bend in the road.* **bends** **2** to become crooked. *Your leg can bend at the knee.* **bends, bent, bending.**

a	hat
ā	age
ä	far
e	let
ē	equal
ėr	term
i	it
ī	ice
o	hot
ō	open
ô	order
oi	oil
ou	out
u	cup
u̇	put
ü	rule
ch	child
ng	long
sh	she
th	thin
ᵀH	then
zh	measure

ə = { a in about
       e in taken
       i in pencil
       o in lemon
       u in circus

balloon

bird /bėrd/ an animal that has feathers, wings, and two legs. The female bird can lay eggs. *A robin is a kind of bird.* **birds.**

blank /blangk/ **1** a space that is not filled in. *Leave a blank if you don't know the answer.* **2** a paper with spaces to be filled in. *Fill in the blanks with the answers.* **blanks.**

blan ket /blang′kit/ a heavy covering made of cloth that keeps people warm. *The mother put a blanket over the child.* **blankets.**

blast /blast/ **1** a big rush of wind. *The open door let in a blast of very cold air.* **2** a very loud sound. *Did you hear the blast of the trumpet?* **blasts.**

blast off /blast off/ to take off into space. *You can see fire when the rockets blast off.* **blasts, blasted, blasting.**

blaze /blāz/ **1** a fire; bright flame. *People could*

bird

blastoff

see the blaze of the burning house from far away. **blazes.** **2** to burn with a bright fire. *See the fire blaze in the fireplace.* **blazes, blazed, blazing.**

blend /blend/ to mix together so you cannot tell one thing from another. *If you blend yellow and blue paints, you will get green.* **blends, blended, blending.**

blimp /blimp/ an airship that is lifted by a very large balloon. **blimps.**

blink /blingk/ to open and shut the eyes quickly. *All people blink several times a minute.* **blinks, blinked, blinking.**

block /blok/ 1 a solid piece of something, such as wood or stone. *The block of ice began to melt.* 2 a part of a city that is closed in by four streets. *Neighbors are people who live on your block.* **blocks.**

blow /blō/ 1 to send out air sharply. *Try to blow out all the birthday candles.* 2 to move with speed or power. *Strong winds can blow down trees.* **blows, blew, blowing.**

boat /bōt/ something that people use to travel on the water. *We rode the boat to the other side of the lake.* **boats.**

book /bůk/ sheets of printed paper bound together between covers. *He has a new book about animals.* **books.**

boot /büt/ a covering for the foot and part of the leg. *He lost a boot in the snow.* **boots.**

brag /brag/ to talk too highly about one's own self or what one owns. *Ted likes to brag about his speed bike.* **brags, bragged, bragging.**

bread /bred/ a baked food made with flour and milk or water. *We need a loaf of bread.* **breads.**

brick /brik/ a block of baked clay, used to make the walls of buildings. **bricks.**

bright /brīt/ 1 giving a lot of light; shining. *Look how bright the stars are tonight.* 2 smart or clever. *The bright boy learns his lessons quickly.* **brighter, brightest.**

bring /bring/ to have something or someone come with you. *Please bring me a sharp pencil.* **brings, brought, bringing.**

brook /brůk/ a small, natural stream. *Let's fish in the brook.* **brooks.**

broom /brüm/ a long-handled brush used for sweeping. **brooms.**

bro ther /bruTH'ər/ a boy who has the same father and mother as other children. **brothers.**

bunch /bunch/ a group of like things that are all together. *He gave Mom a bunch of roses.* **bunches.**

a	hat
ā	age
ä	far
e	let
ē	equal
ėr	term
i	it
ī	ice
o	hot
ō	open
ô	order
oi	oil
ou	out
u	cup
ů	put
ü	rule
ch	child
ng	long
sh	she
th	thin
ŦH	then
zh	measure

ə = { a in about
e in taken
i in pencil
o in lemon
u in circus }

boot

cart

bush /bush/ a low-growing plant that often has many branches starting near the ground. **bushes.**

C

came /kām/ past of *come.* See *come. She came to see me last night.*

camp /kamp/ **1** to put up a tent or the like and stay for a while. *We will camp for one week in the woods.* **camps, camped, camping. 2** a group of tents or the like where people live for a while. *Many people like to go to that camp near the lake.* **camps.**

cane /kān/ a long, narrow stick used to help people walk. *The man used a cane during the hike.* **canes.**

cart /kärt/ **1** a large box-like object with two wheels, often pulled by horses and used to carry heavy loads. *The farmer loaded hay into the cart.* **2** a small box-like object with four wheels that is pushed. *I like to push the grocery cart.* **carts.**

cash /kash/ money in the form of dollar bills and coins. *We paid cash for her new bike.*

cast /kast/ **1** to throw. *She cast a stone into the brook.* **2** to choose for a part in a play. *The teacher cast him as Robin Hood in the school play.* **cast, casting. 3** something put into a mold. *His leg is set in a cast.* **casts.**

cat fish /kat′fish′/ a fish that has no scales, and has long feelers around its mouth like a cat's whiskers. *plural:* **catfish** or **catfishes.**

chick /chik/ **1** a baby chicken. **2** a baby bird. **chicks.**

chick en /chik′ən/ **1** a hen or rooster. **chickens.**

child /chīld/ a young girl or boy. *Every child likes to play.* **children.**

catfish

chil dren /chil′drən/
1 young girls and boys. *All children in America can go to school.* **2** the sons and daughters of parents. *The mother has four children.*

chip munk /chip′mungk/ a small, striped animal something like a squirrel. **chipmunks.**

choke /chōk/ to stop the breath of an animal or person. *He began to choke on a fish bone.* **chokes, choked, choking.**

chore /chôr/ some job to do; a task. *Making the beds was their chore every day.* **chores.**

clash /klash/ a loud, harsh noise such as that made by striking metal or ringing bells together that are not in tune. *We heard the clash of the falling pots and pans.* **clashes**

click /klik/ a short, sharp sound. *We heard a click of the key turning in the lock.* **clicks.**

clock /klok/ a machine that measures and shows time. **clocks.**

clown /kloun/ a person who makes people laugh by doing funny things. *She liked the circus clown.* **clowns.**

coach /kōch/ **1** a large carriage with seats inside that was pulled by horses and used before the days of cars. **2** a person who trains sports teams. *My father is a football coach.* **coaches.**

coat /kōt/ a piece of outer clothing with sleeves. **coats.**

come /kum/ **1** to move toward. *Please come over here.* **2** to arrive. *My sister will come home tomorrow.* **comes, came, coming.**

cook book /kük′bük′/ **a** book that tells how to cook different kinds of food. **cookbooks.**

cot /kot/ **a** small bed that is easily folded. **cots.**

a	hat
ā	age
ä	far
e	let
ē	equal
ėr	term
i	it
ī	ice
o	hot
ō	open
ô	order
oi	oil
ou	out
u	cup
ů	put
ü	rule
ch	child
ng	long
sh	she
th	thin
ŦH	then
zh	measure

ə = {
a in about
e in taken
i in pencil
o in lemon
u in circus
}

clown

count /kount/ **1** to tell numbers in order. *She can count up to one hundred.* **2** to add up the sum. *Will you count how many chairs there are in this room?* **counts, counted, counting.**

cow

cow /kou/ a full-grown female of cattle that gives milk. **cows.**

cream /krēm/ the thick part of milk that rises to the top when milk stands for a time. *Butter is made from cream.*

crook /krük/ **1** to bend. *Crook your finger for him to come near.* **2** a person who is not honest. *The crook took the money and ran.* **crooks.**

cross /krôs/ **1** two sticks that go across each other to make a "T" or an "X." **crosses.** **2** to go from one side to the other. *Cross the street when the light turns green.* **crosses, crossed, crossing.**

crown /kroun/ **1** a head

crown

covering for a king or queen, often made of jewels. **crowns.** **2** to make a man a king or a woman a queen. *They will crown the queen today.* **crowns, crowned, crowning.**

cry /krī/ **1** to call out. *"Wait!" the man began to cry.* **cries.** **2** to shed tears. *The child started to cry when the toy broke.* **cries, cried, crying.** **3** a loud shout. *We heard his cry.*

cut /kut/ **1** to use something sharp to make more than one piece. *Cut your meat with a knife.* **cuts, cut, cutting.** **2** an opening in the body made by something sharp. *He put a bandage over the cut.* **cuts.**

D

dark /därk/ **1** having no light. *Day is light; night is dark.* **2** almost black in color. *His belt and tie are dark brown.* **darker, darkest.**

dash /dash/ **1** to throw hard. *The angry man began to dash his books against the wall.* **2** to move in a hurry; rush. *See the horses dash.* **dashes, dashed, dashing.**

dear /dir/ **1** greatly loved. *Her pet dog is dear to her.* **dearer, dearest. 2** a person who is much loved. *"Hello, my dear," said Father.* **dears.**

deep /dēp/ far down from the top. *The child dug a deep hole.* **deeper, deepest.**

deer /dir/ a fast-moving animal that has hoofs. The male deer has horns or antlers. *plural:* **deer.**

desk /desk/ a piece of furniture with a top like a table, used to write on. **desks.**

die /dī/ to lose life; to stop living. *A plant will die if it is not watered.* **dies, died, dying.**

dig /dig/ to use hands, claws, or tools to make a hole in the ground. *They will dig a hole to plant the young tree.* **digs, dug, digging.**

di no saur /dī′nə sôr/ a kind of animal that lived on the earth and died millions of years ago. **dinosaurs.**

dirt /dėrt/ something such as mud or dust that makes a thing or person dirty. *The football players had dirt on their clothes.*

dish /dish/ something used for holding food, such as a cup, plate, or bowl. **dishes.**

dock /dok/ a raised, flat place built on or from the shore. *The boat was tied to the dock.* **docks.**

does /duz/ a form of *do;* to act, or to carry out a job. *He does the dishes well.*

dog /dôg/ a pet animal with four legs. **dogs.**

dog house /dôg hous′/ a place built outdoors for a dog. **doghouses.**

a	hat
ā	age
ä	far
e	let
ē	equal
ėr	term
i	it
ī	ice
o	hot
ō	open
ô	order
oi	oil
ou	out
u	cup
u̇	put
ü	rule
ch	child
ng	long
sh	she
th	thin
ŦH	then
zh	measure

ə = {
a in about
e in taken
i in pencil
o in lemon
u in circus

deer

down /doun/ to a place below another. *Please put the box down here.*

down town /doun'toun'/ the main part of a town or city where there are stores and offices. *Let's go downtown to the store.*

dream /drēm/ something that is seen during sleep. *I had a wonderful dream last night about a magic cat.* **dreams.**

dress /dres/ a piece of clothing that women and girls wear, made up of a skirt and a top. **dresses.**

drip /drip/ to fall in drops. *Water began to drip from the wet socks.* **drips, dripped, dripping.**

drive /drīv/ **1** to make something leave or go. *Drive the goat away from the garbage.* **2** to run a car, a bus, or other things. *Mom will drive the car.* **drives, drove, driving.**

drove /drōv/ past of *drive.*

drums

See *drive. He drove the bus well.*

drum /drum/ a musical instrument used to sound out the beat of a song. **drums.**

dry /drī/ not wet. *Your swimsuit will be dry in an hour.* **drier, driest.**

duck /duk/ a swimming bird that has webbed feet and short legs. **ducks.**

dump /dump/ **1** to unload; throw down. *The truck began to dump the dirt along the road.* **dumps, dumped, dumping.** **2** a place to throw trash. *Take the old tire to the city dump.* **dumps.**

dust /dust/ very small, dry bits of earth or other material. *There was dust in every room.*

dye /dī/ **1** something used to color cloth, hair, and other things. *The spy used black dye to color his red hair.* **dyes. 2** to color something by dipping it into a dye. *She*

duck

will dye the dress yellow.
dyes, dyed, dyeing.

E

each /ēch/ every one of. *Each child has a hat.*

egg /eg/ **1** that which is laid by a mother bird, or some other female animals. *The baby robin hatched from the egg today.* **2** what is inside a hen's egg, used for food. *That girl eats a boiled egg for lunch.* **eggs.**

eight /āt/ the number that is one more than seven; 8. **eights.**

eve ry /ev′rē/ each one of the whole group. *The cat ate every piece of fish.*

eve ry where /ev′rē where/ in every place; in all places. *People everywhere have feelings like yours and mine.*

eye /ī/ **1** the part of the body that people and animals use for seeing. **2** the colored part of the eye. *My brother has one blue eye and one brown eye.* **eyes.**

F

fam i ly /fam′ə lē/ **1** parents and their children. *We have six people in our family.* **2** all the people one is related to. *Everyone in the family went to my father's birthday party last Sunday.* **families.**

farm /färm/ land on which a person raises animals or grows crops. *There are three barns on that farm.* **farms.**

fast /fast/ **1** quick; having speed. *She is a fast swimmer.* **2** tight. *He has a fast hold of the rope.*

fa ther /fä′ŦHər/ a man who has children. *My father works downtown.* **fathers.**

fed /fed/ past of *feed;* to give food. *The farmer fed corn to the pigs.*

a	hat
ā	age
ä	far
e	let
ē	equal
ėr	term
i	it
ī	ice
o	hot
ō	open
ô	order
oi	oil
ou	out
u	cup
ů	put
ü	rule
ch	child
ng	long
sh	she
th	thin
ŦH	then
zh	measure

ə = {
  a in about
  e in taken
  i in pencil
  o in lemon
  u in circus
}

farm

fish

flock

fight /fīt/ **1** an angry quarrel between two or more people. *The children had a fight over the toy.* **fights.** **2** to take part in a fight. *It is better to talk it over than to fight.* **fights, fought, fighting.**

find /fīnd/ **1** to come upon. *She will find the key.* **2** to learn. *I find I like my new friends better every day.* **finds, found, finding.**

fire pole /fīr′pōl′/ a pole that fire fighters slide down when the fire alarm sounds. **firepoles.**

first /fėrst/ coming in front of or before others. *Who is first in line?*

fish /fish/ a water animal that has gills for breathing and is usually covered with scales. *plural:* **fish** or **fishes.**

five /fīv/ the number that is one more than four; 5. *A person has five fingers on one hand.* **fives.**

fix /fix/ **1** to make something right. *He was able to fix the broken toy.* **2** to make something firm or take hold. *She must fix the telephone number in her mind.* **fixes, fixed, fixing.** **3** a hard place to get out of. *We were in a fix when it rained on our food.* **fixes.**

flash /flash/ **1** a sudden light or flame that lasts a short time. *Thunder followed the flash of light.* **2** a sudden feeling. *He had a flash of hope.* **flashes.**

float /flōt/ to stay on top of water or air. *At the lake, I can float on my back.* **floats, floated, floating.**

flock /flok/ a group of animals of one kind which stay together. *The flock of birds flew south.* **flocks.**

flop /flop/ **1** to move in a loose or heavy way. *I saw the fish flop about on the grass.* **2** to fall or move in a heavy or clumsy way. *The tired girl was ready to flop into a* *chair.* **flops, flopped, flopping.**

fly[1] /flī/ a small bug that has two wings. *There is a fly on your arm.* **flies.**

fly[2] /flī/ to move through the air with wings. *Many birds fly south in winter.* **flies, flew, flying.**

fog /fog/ a cloud near the ground. *It is easy to become lost in thick fog.*

food /füd/ that which people and animals eat in order to live and grow. *We gave food to the hungry people.* **foods.**

foot /fůt/ **1** the part of the body at the end of the leg used for standing on. *Does the shoe fit your foot?* **2** a measure of 12 inches. **feet.**

foot ball /fůt′bôl′/ **1** a sport played with a ball which is kicked, passed, or carried past a line at either end of a playing field. **2** the ball used in this sport. **footballs.**

for /for/ or /fər/ **1** in place of. *We used a stick for a bat.* **2** to belong to. *The books are for us.* **3** as long as. *They worked on the farm for ten days.* **4** to get to. *The big bus left for New York.*

found /found/ past of *find.* See *find. We found our lost cat.*

four /fôr/ the number that is one more than three; 4. *A cow has four legs.* **fours.**

free /frē/ **1** not being under someone's power. *A slave is not a free person.* **2** to set loose. *She is going to free the animal caught in the trap.* **frees, freed, freeing. 3** costing nothing. *That store gives free tastes of food.*

friend /frend/ a person who knows and likes another person. *Jamie is her best friend at school.* **friends.**

frisk y /fris′kē/ full of fun and life. *The frisky puppy played and jumped.* **friskier, friskiest.**

a	hat
ā	age
ä	far
e	let
ē	equal
ėr	term
i	it
ī	ice
o	hot
ō	open
ô	order
oi	oil
ou	out
u	cup
ů	put
ü	rule
ch	child
ng	long
sh	she
th	thin
ŦH	then
zh	measure

ə = {
a in about
e in taken
i in pencil
o in lemon
u in circus

fly

frog /frôg/ a small jumping animal that has webbed feet and lives in the water or near it. **frogs.**

frog

front /frunt/ **1** the first part. *The first child in a line is at the front.* **2** the part that faces straight ahead. *Most shirts button down the front.* **fronts.**

full /fùl/ the opposite of empty; filled up to the top. *She had a full glass of milk.* **fuller, fullest.**

G

gas /gas/ **1** matter that has no shape, can become bigger without end, and might not be seen. *There are many gases in the air.* **2** short for *gasoline,* a fuel for cars, buses, and the like. **gases.**

get /get/ to receive or reach. *I like to get presents. He will get there on time.* **gets, got** or **gotten, getting.**

girl

girl /gėrl/ a young female person from birth to about eighteen years old. **girls.**

give /giv/ **1** to hand over as a present. *Mother will give us apples after school.* **2** to hand over a thing. *Please give me the salt.* **gives, gave, giving.**

glad /glad/ happy; having joy. *He was glad to make the team.* **gladder, gladdest.**

glass /glas/ **1** that which windows are made of. **2** something that you use for drinking. **glasses.**

globe /glōb/ **1** the earth. **2** a ball with a map of the earth printed on it. **globes.**

glove /gluv/ something to wear on the hand that has a place for each finger. **gloves.**

glue /glü/ **1** something used to stick things together. *We can mend the plate with glue.* **2** to stick together. *We glued* the three pieces together. **glues, glued, gluing.**

go /gō/ to move or leave. *I go to school by bus.* **goes, went, gone, going.**

goat /gōt/ a sheeplike animal with horns, raised for their milk and their hides. **goats.**

goes /gōz/ a form of *go.* See *go. She goes swimming often.*

good /guḋ/ **1** fine or well done. *He does good work at school.* **2** just as it should be. *This is a good place to make camp.* **3** doing what is right. *A good man does not tell lies.* **better, best.**

goose /güs/ a water bird, like a duck but bigger, with a longer neck. **geese.**

got /got/ a form of *get.* See *get. She got good grades.*

grand /grand/ **1** looking large and fine. *The Mississippi is a grand river.* **2** being fine, important. *The grand old* man helped his country. **grander, grandest.**

grand fa ther /grand′ fä′₣Hər/ the father of a person's father or mother. **grandfathers.**

grand moth er /grand′ mu₣H′ər/ the mother of a person's father or mother. **grandmothers.**

grape /grāp/ a small, round fruit that grows on a vine. Grapes can be red, purple, or green. **grapes.**

grass /gras/ green plants that cover fields and lawns. **grasses.**

gray /grā/ a color between black and white. *Color the sky gray.* **grays.**

grin /grin/ **1** to give a big smile. *He began to grin when he saw his friend.* **grins, grinned, grinning.** **2** a large smile. *Her grin shows that two teeth are missing.* **grins.**

a	hat
ā	age
ä	far
e	let
ē	equal
ėr	term
i	it
ī	ice
o	hot
ō	open
ô	order
oi	oil
ou	out
u	cup
u̇	put
ü	rule
ch	child
ng	long
sh	she
th	thin
₣H	then
zh	measure

ə = { a in about / e in taken / i in pencil / o in lemon / u in circus

grape

grow /grō/ to become bigger in size. *An oak tree can grow from a small seed.* **grows, grew, growing.**

grump /grump/ **1** to talk of not being pleased. *Don't grump about the flat tire.* **grumps, grumped, grumping.** **2** one you cannot please. *She is a grump until noon.* **grumps.**

H

hand /hand/ **1** part of the body at the end of the arm which has four fingers and a thumb. *He caught the ball with one hand.* **2** a thing like a hand. *The big hand of the clock points to three.* **hands.**

hard /härd/ **1** not soft. *The chair is made from a very hard wood.* **2** not easy to do or understand. *These math lessons are hard.* **harder, hardest.**

harm /härm/ **1** a hurt or a loss. *There was no harm* done when the wagon turned over. **2** to hurt. *Cold weather can harm many kinds of flowers.* **harms, harmed, harming.**

has /haz/ a form of *have.* See *have. Who has the letter?*

have /hav/ to hold in one's hand or keep. *I have the paper in my hand.* **has, had, having.**

hay /hā/ food for farm animals that is made from dried grass, alfalfa, or clover.

his /hiz/ belonging to a boy or man. *Tom likes his bike.*

hit /hit/ to strike or give a blow to. *Try to hit the ball with the bat.* **hits, hit, hitting.**

hit ting /hit′ting/ a form of *hit.* See *hit. He is hitting the rug with a broom to clean it.*

hook /hu̇k/ **1** something with a bend on which

hay

hook

174

things can be hung. **2** a bent piece of wire that is sharp at one end and used for catching fish. **hooks.**

hop ping /hop′ping/ a form of *hop*, which means "to jump" *Frogs were hopping in the grass.* **hops, hopped.**

horn /hôrn/ **1** a hard object that grows on the heads of some animals, such as goats and deer. **2** a musical instrument played by blowing. *He plays the horn in the school band.* **3** something that makes a loud noise in order to warn. *He honked the car horn.* **horns.**

horse /hôrs/ a large animal that has four legs, hoofs, a long mane, and a tail. **horses.**

house /hous/ a building that people live in. *Their house has four bedrooms.* **houses.**

howl /houl/ **1** to cry out in a long, loud, and sad way. *Listen to the wind howl.* **2** a cry that is long, loud, and sad. *Do you hear the howl of the wolf?* **howls, howled, howling.**

hush /hush/ to become quiet. *A bottle will make the crying baby hush.* **hushes, hushed, hushing.**

I

if /if/ in case. *If it snows, school will be closed.*

inside /in′sīd′/ the part within. *What's inside the box?*

in to /in′tü/ toward or to the inside. *When you hear the bell, come into school.*

J

jam¹ /jam/ fruit made sweet and cooked until thick. *We put jam on our toast.* **jams.**

jam² /jam/ to press into a small space. *Don't jam your car into that space.* **jams, jammed, jamming.**

a	hat
ā	age
ä	far
e	let
ē	equal
ėr	term
i	it
ī	ice
o	hot
ō	open
ô	order
oi	oil
ou	out
u	cup
u̇	put
ü	rule
ch	child
ng	long
sh	she
th	thin
ŦH	then
zh	measure

ə = { a in about
e in taken
i in pencil
o in lemon
u in circus

horn

kangaroo

kick

job /job/ **1** a bit of work. *She had the job of drying the dishes.* **2** work that a person does for pay from week to week. *She is looking for a job as a teacher.* **jobs.**

jog /jog/ **1** to shake with a push. *The milk will spill if you jog my arm.* **2** to trot or walk slowly. *We like to jog every day.* **jogs, jogged, jogging.**

jump /jump/ **1** to leap from the ground; spring. *She can jump high.* **2** to spring over. *Can you jump the opening in the rocks?* **3** to give a sudden, quick start of the body. *The loud noise made him jump.* **jumps, jumped, jumping.**

just /just/ **1** only. *My house is just a block away.* **2** barely. *He just made the team.*

K

kan ga roo /kan′gə rü′/ an animal that lives in Australia that can jump far and fast, and whose females carry their young in a pocket of skin. **kangaroos.**

kick /kik/ to hit with the foot. *Kick the football.* **kicks, kicked, kicking.**

kind[1] /kīnd/ friendly, doing good, and helping others. *Our doctor is a kind person.*

kind[2] /kīnd/ sort or type. *She likes that kind of fruit best.* **kinds.**

kiss /kis/ **1** to touch with the lips; to show love or good will. *He goes to kiss his aunt goodnight.* **kisses, kissed, kissing.** **2** a touch with the lips that shows love or good will. *May I have a kiss goodbye?* **kisses.**

L

land /land/ **1** the ground. *We use our land for a garden.* **lands** **2** bring to land or put on

176

land. *Will Ted land that big fish?* **lands, landed, landing.**

lap /lap/ the front part of a sitting person's body, from the waist to the knees. **laps.**

last /last/ coming at the end, after all others. *Ted is the last one in line.*

leave /lēv/ to go away. *Ned will leave today.* **leaves, left, leaving.**

light[1] /līt/ **1** not dark; that by which people and animals can see. *We need light.* **2** something that gives light. *Turn off the light when you leave.* **lights.**

light[2] /līt/ not heavy. *A feather is light.* **lighter, lightest.**

li on /lī′ən/ a large jungle cat whose males have full manes of hair. **lions.**

list /list/ a number of names or words in a row. *Here's a list of good books to read.* **lists.**

live /liv/ **1** to have life.

Animals need food, water, and air to live. **2** to make one's home in a certain place. *She will live in New York.* **lives, lived, living.**

lock /lok/ **1** something that keeps a door, box, or window shut, and needs a key to open it. *Will the key fit into the front door lock?* **locks.** **2** to fasten with a lock. *Amy forgot to lock the door when she left.* **locks, locked, locking.**

log /lôg/ a piece of wood from a tree. *Put another log into the fire.* **logs.**

long /lông/ not short; from one end to the other end. *A giraffe has a long neck.* **longer, longest.**

lose /lüz/ to be unable to find. *I hope I don't lose my gloves.* **loses, lost, losing.**

lost /lôst/ a form of *lose.* See *lose.* *I lost my new pencil.*

a	hat
ā	age
ä	far
e	let
ē	equal
ėr	term
i	it
ī	ice
o	hot
ō	open
ô	order
oi	oil
ou	out
u	cup
ù	put
ü	rule
ch	child
ng	long
sh	she
th	thin
ŦH	then
zh	measure

ə = {
a in about
e in taken
i in pencil
o in lemon
u in circus

lion

lot /lot/ **1** a great many; much. *She has a lot of toys.* **2** a plot of ground. *He built a house on the lot.* **lots.**

loud /loud/ making a large sound; not soft. *A drum can make a loud sound.* **louder, loudest.**

luck /luk/ that which seems to happen by chance. *With good luck, it won't rain on our picnic.*

lunch /lunch/ the meal eaten between breakfast and dinner. *Would you like a sandwich for lunch?* **lunches.**

lunch box /lunch'boks/ a box for holding and carrying one's meal. **lunchboxes.**

map

M

mad /mad/ angry. *Father got mad when the dog ate his shoes.* **madder, maddest.**

man /man/ a grown-up male person; what a boy

mask

grows up to be. *My father is a tall man.* **men.**

man y /men'ē/ a large number of. *There are many animals at the zoo.*

map /map/ a drawing of part of the earth, showing where the countries, cities, rivers, seas, lakes, and mountains are. **maps.**

march /märch/ **1** to walk and step in time. *Everyone in the circus parade began to march down the street.* **marches, marched, marching.** **2** music for marching. *A march makes you feel good.* **marches.**

mask /mask/ a covering for the face with openings for the eyes. *What mask will you wear on Halloween?* **masks.**

meal /mēl/ breakfast, lunch, dinner, or supper; food eaten at one time. *We ate a good meal before the hike.* **meals.**

mean[1] /mēn/ to have in mind. *What do you mean*

by that? **means, meant, meaning.**

mean² /mēn/ not kind. *It is mean to make fun of other people.* **meaner, meanest.**

meat /mēt/ food that comes from animals. *Hamburger is meat.* **meats.**

meet /mēt/ **1** to come face to face with. *I hope I meet my friend downtown.* **2** join. *Your arm and your body meet at the shoulder.* **meets, met, meeting.**

mend /mend/ to fix; to put something in good shape. *Father will mend the broken chair.* **mends, mended, mending.**

mess /mess/ **1** a state in which things are dirty or not neat. *Mother made him clean the mess in his room.* **messes. 2** to make dirty or not neat. *Do not let the puppy mess up the living room!* **messes, messed, messing.**

met /met/ past of *meet.*

See *meet. I met my dad in the park last night.*

might¹ /mīt/ could. Past of *may.* See *may. We might go if it's sunny.*

might² /mīt/ great strength or power. *Press down with all your might.*

milk /milk/ **1** a white liquid which we drink that comes from cows. *May I have some milk?* **2** get milk from a cow. *Help him milk the cows.* **milks, milked, milking.**

mi nus /mī′nəs/ fewer than. *Three minus one is two.*

mitt /mit/ a glove used for catching a baseball. *The catcher always wears a mitt.* **mitts.**

mix /miks/ **1** to stir. *We need to mix the milk into the batter.* **2** to put together. *Mix the boys and girls in each class.* **mixes, mixed, mixing. 3** food that has been put together. *Here's a box of cake mix.* **mixes.**

milk

moose

nest

moon /mün/ a body in the sky which is usually seen at night. **moons.**

moose /müs/ a large animal in the deer family. *plural:* **moose.**

mop /mop/ **1** a stick with cloth at the end used for cleaning. *Use the mop to clean up the water.* **mops.** **2** to clean up. *Mop the floor.* **mops, mopped, mopping.**

mopped /mopt/ past of *mop.* See *mop. We mopped up the milk that had spilled.*

more /môr/ **1** a greater amount or number. *There are more boys than girls in our class.* **2** an extra amount or number. *Please give me more milk.*

morn ing /môr′ning/ the part of the day that ends at noon. *I like to get up early in the morning.* **mornings.**

moth er /muŦH′ər/ the female parent. *I call my mother Mom.* **mothers.**

much /much/ a large amount. *There is much sand at the beach.* **more, most.**

mud /mud/ very wet, soft dirt. *There is mud in my yard after it rains.*

must /must/ **1** to have to. *We must keep the door closed so the cat will not get out.* **2** should. *You must see that movie.*

N

nest /nest/ **1** a home made by birds in which they lay eggs. *The robins made a nest in the old oak tree in my yard.* **2** a place where other animals live. *The squirrels had a nest in the tree.* **nests.**

night /nīt/ time of day between evening and morning, usually when it's dark. *I like to watch the stars at night.* **nights.**

nine /nīn/ the number that is one more than

eight and one less than ten; 9. **nines.**

note book /nōt′bŭk′/ a book in which to write notes. *I write my homework in my notebook.* **notebooks.**

now /nou/ at or by this time. *He is ready now.*

num ber /num′bər/ **1** the sum of a group of things. *The number of books I have read this year is nine.* **2** a word that tells how many. *Ten is a number.* **numbers.** **3** to give a number to. *After I wrote my book, I had to number the pages.* **numbers, numbered, numbering.**

O

off /ôf/ **1** away from a usual place. *I took my mittens off.* **2** away from. *They are off on a trip.* **3** to stop. *Turn the water off.* **4** loose. *The button is almost off.*

one /wun/ **1** the number 1. **2** a single person or thing. *Pick the one you like best.* **ones** **3** a person who stands for people in general. *One must try hard.*

ouch /ouch/ word said when a person is hurt.

out /out/ **1** away from. *Come out of the pool now.* **2** not in a usual place. *We are out of our room.* **3** not in use. *The lights are out.* **4** lacking; without. *We are out of paper.*

owl /oul/ a bird with a short beak which usually flies and hunts at night. **owls.**

P

pack /pak/ **1** things that are put or tied together. *I carry my books in a pack.* **packs.** **2** to fill with. *I pack my lunch in a paper bag.* **3** to put together or press closely together. *Pack the leaves in this can.* **packs, packed, packing.**

a	hat
ā	age
ä	far
e	let
ē	equal
ėr	term
i	it
ī	ice
o	hot
ō	open
ô	order
oi	oil
ou	out
u	cup
u̇	put
ü	rule
ch	child
ng	long
sh	she
th	thin
ŦH	then
zh	measure

ə = {
a in about
e in taken
i in pencil
o in lemon
u in circus
}

owl

peaches

pine

pail /pāl/ a round holder for sand or water. **pails.**

pain /pān/ **1** a feeling of hurt. *I had a pain in my knee after I fell.* **pains.** **2** to give hurt or pain. *Does your foot still pain you?* **pains, pained, paining.**

par ent /per′ənt/ or /par′ənt/ mother or father. *Have either parent sign this note.* **parents.**

park /pärk/ **1** an open space, with grass and trees, for everyone. **parks.** **2** to leave a car for a time. *Park the car on the street.* **parks, parked, parking.**

past /past/ **1** ended. *Winter is past.* **2** farther on than. *She ran past me early in the race.* **3** time gone by. *I like to read about life in the past.*

pat /pat/ to touch lightly, usually with the hand. *Pat the kitten gently.* **pats, patted, patting.**

path /path/ a road, not usually a wide one. **paths.**

peach /pēch/ a yellow-pink fruit with a fuzzy skin which grows on a tree. **peaches.**

pen[1] /pen/ something used to write with using ink. **pens.**

pen[2] /pen/ **1** a small yard for animals such as pigs. **pens.** **2** to shut in closely. *Pen the chicks in the barn.* **pens, penned, penning.**

per son /pėr′sən/ a man, woman, girl, or boy. *Each person should help out.*

pin /pin/ **1** a small, thin pointed piece of metal used to hold things together. **pins.** **2** to put on with a pin. *Pin the curtain back.* **pins, pinned, pinning.**

pine[1] /pīn/ a tree that has pine cones and small leaves that look like needles. **pines.**

pine[2] /pīn/ wish or long

for. *After I move, I am going to pine for my old friends.* **pines, pined, pining.**

plan /plan/ **1** a way of doing something which has been worked out ahead of time. *We made a plan to cook breakfast for my father.* **plans. 2** to work something out ahead of time. *We plan to go out tonight.* **plans, planned, planning.**

plan et /plan′it/ a body in the sky which moves around the sun, such as Jupiter or Earth. **planets.**

plate /plāt/ **1** something to put food on; a dish. **2** in baseball, home base. **plates.**

plot /plot/ **1** a small piece of land. *She grew beans in a plot in her yard.* **2** a secret plan. *We made a plot to surprise our dad.* **3** the main idea of a book. *If I tell you the plot, the book won't be fun.* **plots. 4** to make a

secret plan. *They plot a surprise for their parents.* **plots, plotted, plotting.**

plum /plum/ a round fruit with a smooth skin. **plums.**

plus /plus/ **1** in addition to. *Three plus two is five.* **2** the sign +, meaning "in addition to." *Three + two is five.* **3** and also. *I have an apple plus a pear.*

poke /pōk/ to push, often with something pointed. *Don't poke me with your elbow.* **pokes, poked, poking.**

pond /pond/ body of water smaller than a lake. **ponds.**

pool[1] /pül/ a tank of water to swim in. **pools.**

pool[2] /pül/ things put together, such as money or people. *Our fathers take turns driving in the car pool.* **pools.**

pull /pùl/ to move by tugging toward oneself. *Pull the door shut.* **pulls, pulled, pulling.**

a	hat
ā	age
ä	far
e	let
ē	equal
ėr	term
i	it
ī	ice
o	hot
ō	open
ô	order
oi	oil
ou	out
u	cup
ù	put
ü	rule
ch	child
ng	long
sh	she
th	thin
ŦH	then
zh	measure

ə = { a in about / e in taken / i in pencil / o in lemon / u in circus

pool

push /pȯsh/ **1** to move by pressing away. *Push the swing to make it go high.* **pushes, pushed, pushing. 2** the act of pushing. *Give the cart a push.* **pushes.**

QR

rab bit /rab′it/ an animal with soft fur and long ears that moves by jumping. **rabbits.**

raise /rāz/ **1** to lift up. *Raise your hand if you want to answer.* **2** to put higher. *Raise the flag.* **raises, raised, raising.**

rake /rāk/ **1** a tool with a long handle used for gathering leaves or hay. **rakes. 2** to move with a rake. *Rake up the leaves.* **rakes, raked, raking.**

ram /ram/ **1** a male sheep. **rams. 2** to hit hard. *I saw the ball ram against the wall.* **rams, rammed, ramming.**

reach /rēch/ **1** to get to. *I hope my letter will reach you soon.* **2** to stretch out to; touch. *Can you reach the top shelf?* **reaches, reached, reaching.**

rest[1] /rest/ **1** to be still or quiet after working. *She took a rest after working.* **rests, rested, resting. 2** sleep. *Have a good night's rest.*

rest[2] /rest/ part that is left. *She ate the rest of the apple.*

rich /rich/ having a lot of money or goods. *Rich people can buy whatever they want.* **richer, richest.**

right /rīt/ **1** good; correct. *You did the right thing.* **2** opposite of left. *Give me your right hand.*

rip /rip/ **1** to tear apart or off. *Rip open the box.* **rips, ripped, ripping. 2** a torn place. *I will sew the rip in my coat.* **rips.**

rake

road /rōd/ a place for cars and trucks to travel on; a street **roads.**

rob in /rob′ən/ a bird with brown feathers and a reddish breast. **robins.**

rock[1] /rok/ a large stone or a piece of stone. **rocks.**

rock[2] /rok/ to move back and forth or from side to side. *The waves will rock this small boat.* **rocks, rocked, rocking.**

rode /rōd/ past of *ride;* to be carried on or along on. *We rode our horses up the hill.*

room /rüm/ **1** part of a building with walls of its own. *A kitchen is the room for cooking.* **rooms.** **2** space. *Is there room for me on the bench?*

row /rō/ **1** to move a boat with oars. *Row the boat to shore.* **rows, rowed, rowing.** **2** a line of people or things. *The chairs are in a row.* **rows.**

rub /rub/ to move something back and forth on something else. *Rub your hands with soap.* **rubs, rubbed, rubbing.**

rude /rüd/ not polite. *It is rude to turn your back when someone is talking.* **ruder, rudest.**

rug /rug/ a floor covering made of wool, fur, or rags. **rugs.**

run /run/ go by moving the legs fast; go in a hurry. *I can run to that tree in ten seconds.* **runs, ran, running.**

run ning /run ing/ form of *run.* See *run. We are running to catch the bus.*

rush /rush/ to go in a hurry or with speed. *I have to rush to be on time.* **rushes, rushed, rushing.**

rust /rust/ a reddish brown covering on iron or steel when it has been wet or has become old.

robin

185

S

sack /sak/ a large bag made of paper or other material. *Put the apples in the sack.* **sacks.**

sail boat /sāl′bōt′/ a boat that is moved by the wind blowing against sails. **sailboats.**

sand /sand/ tiny pieces of worn-down rock. *She plays in the sand at the beach.*

sandbox

sand box /sand′boks′/ a box filled with sand for children to play in. *My brother plays in the sandbox at the park.* **sandboxes.**

say /sā/ to speak; put into words. *Can you say which one is better?* **says, said, saying.**

sea /sē/ a large body of salt water such as the Red Sea or North Sea. **seas.**

seal¹ /sēl/ a sea animal with flippers. **seals.**

seal

seal² /sēl/ to close tightly.

Seal the letter before you mail it. **seals, sealed, sealing.**

seam /sēm/ the line formed by sewing together two pieces of cloth. *My dress has a seam in the back.* **seams.**

sec ond¹ /sec′ənd/ **1** the place between first and third. *I am second in line.* **2** another. *He had a second glass of milk?*

sec ond² /sec′ənd/ one of 60 short periods of time in an hour. **seconds.**

see /sē/ **1** to look at. *See the moon!* **2** to find out. *We will see about that.* **sees, saw, seen, seeing.**

seem /sēm/ to appear to be; look like. *Does the answer seem to be right to you?* **seems, seemed, seeming.**

seen /sēn/ past of *see*. See *see*. *Have you seen who just came in?* **seen, saw, seeing.**

send /send/ to make something go from one

place to another. *Send the letter by air mail.* **sends, sent, sending.**

sev en /sev′ən/ the number between six and eight; 7. **sevens.**

shack /shak/ a small house or cabin which is usually not in good shape. *There is a shack in back of the house.* **shacks.**

shad ow /shad′ō/ shade made by a person or thing. *The boy's shadow is on the wall.* **shadows.**

shake /shāk/ to move back and forth or up and down. *Shake your head when you know the answer.* **shakes, shook, shaking**

shall /shal/ used to tell of future time. *We shall certainly call when we get there.* **should.**

shame /shām/ **1** a feeling of having done something wrong. *It was a shame I broke the plate.* **2** to make someone feel shame. *Don't shame me in front of my friends.* **shames, shamed, shaming.**

share /sher/ or /shar/ **1** a part or portion. *I'll do my share of the work.* **shares.** **2** to divide into parts. *Please share the apple with the others.* **shares, shared, sharing.**

shark /shärk/ a large, dangerous fish with sharp teeth. **sharks.**

sharp /shärp/ having a point and/or a thin cutting edge. *The sharp knife sliced the cheese.* **sharper, sharpest.**

sheep /shēp/ an animal with a furry coat that is used to make wool. *plural:* **sheep.**

shine /shīn/ **1** light. *The shine of the sun hurts my eyes.* **2** to polish. *I need to shine my old shoes.* **shines, shone** or **shined, shining.** **3** good weather. *The mail comes rain or shine.* **4** to be bright. *The silver pin had a bright shine.*

a	hat
ā	age
ä	far
e	let
ē	equal
ėr	term
i	it
ī	ice
o	hot
ō	open
ô	order
oi	oil
ou	out
u	cup
ù	put
ü	rule
ch	child
ng	long
sh	she
th	thin
ŦH	then
zh	measure

ə = { a in about
e in taken
i in pencil
o in lemon
u in circus }

shadow

187

shirt

shore

shirt /shèrt/ clothing worn on the upper part of the body. **shirts.**

shock /shok/ **1** a surprise, sudden noise, or crash. *His leaving early was a shock.* **shocks. 2** to make someone feel surprise or anger. **shocks, shocked, shocking.**

shook /shůk/ past of *shake.* See *shake. We shook hands when we met.*

shoot /shüt/ **1** to send quickly. *Shoot the ball over to me.* **2** to take a picture. *I will shoot when everyone is ready.* **shoots, shot, shooting.**

shore /shôr/ land at the edge of a river, sea, or lake. *Dig in the sand near the shore.* **shores.**

short /shôrt/ **1** not tall. *He is too short to reach it.* **2** not long. *It is a short time until dinner.* **shorter, shortest.**

shut /shut/ **1** to close.

Tell Amy to shut the door. **2** to keep in. *Shut the cat up in the house.* **shuts, shut, shutting.**

shy /shī/ bashful; easily frightened. *She was shy with new people.* **shyer, shyest.**

sick /sik/ in bad health; not well. *Stay in bed when you are sick.* **sicker, sickest.**

sight /sīt/ **1** something to see. *The big bridge is a pretty sight.* **2** act of seeing. *His sight is perfect.* **3** something seen. *The first sight of the food made me hungry.* **sights.**

sister /sis′tər/ a girl who has the same parents as other children. *My sister is a year older than I.* **sisters.**

six /siks/ the number that is one more than five; half a dozen; 6. **sixes.**

skip /skip/ **1** to jump lightly. *Let's skip to the music.* **2** to leave out. *You may skip the* story *if you have already read it.* **skips, skipped, skipping.**

skip ping /skip′ing/ form of *skip.* See *skip. The girls are skipping rope. Skipping breakfast is not a good idea.*

slam /slam/ to close with a bang or force. *Try not to slam the door.* **slams, slammed, slamming.**

slant /slant/ slope. *The roof has a sharp slant so snow will fall off it.* **slants.**

sled /sled/ a wooden seat on runners to use on snow or ice. **sleds.**

sleep /slēp/ **1** a rest of the body and mind. *Go to sleep early.* **2** to rest the body and mind. *I like to sleep with a light on.* **sleeps, slept, sleeping.**

sleet /slēt/ rain mixed with snow or ice. *Sleet makes the roads slippery.*

slick /slik/ smooth and slippery. *Slick ice is best for skating.* **slicker, slickest.**

slide /slīd/ to move easily and smoothly. *I like to slide down hills on my sled.* **slides, slid, sliding.**

slip /slip/ **1** to slide suddenly. *I walked slowly so I wouldn't slip on the ice.* **2** to go easily. *Slip into line quietly.* **slips, slipped, slipping.**

slot /slot/ a small, narrow opening. **slots.**

slow /slō/ **1** taking a long time; not fast. *That is the slow train.* **2** in a slow way. *Go slow!* **slower, slowest.**

sly /slī/ able to fool or trick; tricky. *The sly fox was able to trick the rabbit.* **slyer, slyest.**

smart[1] /smart/ clever; bright. *You will do well if you are smart.* **smarter, smartest.**

smart[2] /smart/ to hurt or sting. *Does that cut smart?* **smarts, smarted, smarting.**

a	hat
ā	age
ä	far
e	let
ē	equal
ėr	term
i	it
ī	ice
o	hot
ō	open
ô	order
oi	oil
ou	out
u	cup
ù	put
ü	rule
ch	child
ng	long
sh	she
th	thin
ŦH	then
zh	measure

ə = { a in about
e in taken
i in pencil
o in lemon
u in circus }

slide

snack /snak/ a small meal; something to eat. *I like to have an apple for a snack after school.* **snacks.**

snake /snāk/ **1** a long, thin, crawling animal with no legs. **snakes. 2** to wind like a snake. *The road has to snake along the river.* **snakes, snaked, snaking.**

snake

sneeze /snēz/ **1** to push air quickly and suddenly from the nose and mouth. *Sometimes flowers make my friend sneeze.* **sneezes, sneezed, sneezing. 2** the act of sneezing. *I never have just one sneeze.* **sneezes.**

snow /snō/ **1** soft flakes of frozen water which fall from clouds. *It's fun to play in the snow.* **2** the fall of snow. *It will snow all day today.* **snows, snowed, snowing.**

soap /sōp/ something used to wash with. *Wash your hands with soap.*

sog gy /sog′ē/ very wet. *The papers got soggy from the rain.* **soggier, soggiest.**

snow

some thing /sum′thing/ a particular thing not named. *Please give me something to eat.*

song /sông/ something to sing. *Can you sing another song?* **songs.**

soon /sün/ in a short while. *We will meet again soon.*

sound[1] /sound/ **1** that which can be heard. *I like the sound of music.* **sounds. 2** to make a sound. *The bells sound every hour.* **sounds, sounded, sounding.**

sound[2] /sound/ healthy. *The tree is sound.*

south /south/ direction opposite north, to the left as one faces the setting sun.

space /spās/ **1** a large, open amount of room. *Rockets go into space.* **2** a certain amount of room. *There is space next to me.* **spaces.**

spark /spärk/ a small piece of fire. *Just one spark can start a fire.* **sparks.**

speak /spēk/ to talk. *I will speak to you on the telephone later.* **speaks, spoke, spoken, speaking.**

speech /spēch/ **1** the act of talking. *A child learns speech at an early age.* **2** what is said when a person speaks. *We heard a speech on rockets.* **speeches.**

speed /spēd/ **1** quick, rapid movement. *The car was going at a high rate of speed.* **2** go faster than is safe. *Don't speed!* **speeds, sped** or **speeded, speeding.**

spin /spin/ **1** to turn or make turn quickly. *It's fun to watch a top spin.* **2** to make a web. **spins, spun, spinning.**

spoke¹ /spōk/ past of *speak.* See *speak. She spoke about her trip.* **speaking.**

spoke² /spōk/ one of the bars on a wheel which goes from the center to the rim. **spokes.**

spoon /spün/ a small bowl with a handle that is used to eat with. **spoons.**

spot /spot/ **1** a small mark that does not come off. *He has a spot on his shirt.* **2** a place. *This is a good spot for a picnic.* **spots.**

spy /spī/ **1** a person who watches others secretly. **spies. 2** to be a spy. *He tries to spy on his older brother.* **spies, spied, spying.**

stack /stak/ **1** a large, high pile of hay, books, or wood. **stacks. 2** to put something into a stack. *Stack the wood next to the door.* **stacks, stacked, stacking.**

stain /stān/ a spot or mark. *Try not to get a stain on your new pants.* **stains.**

spoon

stamp

stem

stamp /stamp/ **1** a small piece of paper with a sticky back, that is put on a letter. **stamps. 2** to put a stamp on a letter. *Make sure you stamp that before you mail it.* **stamps, stamped, stamping.**

stand /stand/ **1** to be on one's feet; be upright. *We stand when the flag is raised.* **2** be in a certain place. *The desk can stand by the door.* **stands, stood, standing.**

stem /stem/ the part of a plant or flower which is above ground to which the leaves are attached. **stems.**

stick[1] /stik/ a small, thin piece of wood or other material. **sticks.**

stick[2] /stik/ to put on; attach. *Stick the stamp on the letter.* **sticks, stuck, sticking.**

sting /sting/ **1** to be hurt or pricked by a sharp point, especially by a bee or wasp. **stings. 2** to hurt from a sting. *My finger still stings.* **stings, stung, stinging.**

stood /stùd/ past of *stand.* See *stand. They stood waiting for the parade to begin.* **stood.**

store /stôr/ **1** a place where things are sold. **stores. 2** to keep things for later use. *Store the masks in this box for next Halloween.* **stores, stored, storing.**

stripe /strīp/ a long, thin band of color. *A skunk has a stripe down its back.* **stripes.**

stuck /stuk/ past of *stick.* See *stick. The papers were stuck together.*

T

take /tāk/ to go with; carry. *She will take her book to school.* **takes, took, taking.**

tap /tap/ to hit or touch

lightly. *Tap his arm.*
taps, tapped, tapping.

tapped /tapt/ past of *tap.*
See *tap. She began to tap
on my window to call me.*

task /task/ job; work to be
done. *My task is to clean
my room.* **tasks.**

teach /tēch/ to help one to
learn or understand. *Can
you teach me how to draw
faces?* **teaches, taught,
teaching.**

team /tēm/ a group of two
or more people or
animals working
together. *I help my team
by trying hard.* **teams.**

ten /ten/ the number
which is one more than
nine; 10. **tens.**

test /test/ **1** a way to see
if someone knows
something. *I do well on a
spelling test.* **tests. 2** to
give a test. *The teacher
will test us in math.*
tests, tested, testing.

thank /thangk/ to say one

is pleased about
something. *I am going to
thank my friends for the
present.* **thanks,
thanked, thanking.**

thick /thik/ with much
room from one side to the
opposite side; not thin.
1 *The walls are thick.* **2**
set close together. *She
has thick hair.* **thicker,
thickest.**

thin /thin/ **1** with little
room from one side to the
opposite side; not thick.
*Use a thin wire to hang the
picture.* **2** not fat. *I
want to always eat well
and stay thin.* **thinner,
thinnest.**

thing /thing/ an object;
something that can be
seen, smelled, or touched.
*Give me that thing in
your hand.* **things.**

think /thingk/ **1** to use
the mind. *Think before
you speak.* **2** to believe.
I think it will snow.
**thinks, thought,
thinking.**

a	hat
ā	age
ä	far
e	let
ē	equal
ėr	term
i	it
ī	ice
o	hot
ō	open
ô	order
oi	oil
ou	out
u	cup
ů	put
ü	rule
ch	child
ng	long
sh	she
th	thin
ᵀH	then
zh	measure

ə = {
a in about
e in taken
i in pencil
o in lemon
u in circus
}

193

third /thėrd/ **1** the next after second. *Jane was first, Bill second, and Penny third.* **2** three equal parts. **thirds.**

three /thrē/ the number which is one more than two; 3. **threes.**

ti ger /tī′gər/ a large, animal in the cat family. It has stripes and yellowish fur. **tigers.**

tight /tīt/ not loose; firmly held. *My belt is too tight.* **tighter, tightest.**

tip[1] /tip/ the part at the end. *I can reach it with the tip of my fingers.* **tips.**

tip[2] /tip/ turn over. *Be careful you don't tip over your milk.* **tips, tipped, tipping.**

to /tü/, /tu̇/, or /tə/ **1** to go in the direction of. *Go to the corner.* **2** for. *My aunt came to visit me.* **3** about. *What will he say to that?* **4** *to* is used with action words. *She likes to sew.*

toad /tōd/ a small animal

tiger

toad

like a frog which lives on the ground, not in water. **toads.**

toast /tōst/ **1** bread which has been browned by heat. **2** to make toast. *Please toast this bread lightly.* **toasts, toasted, toasting.**

to geth er /tə geTH′ər/ **1** with another. *They like to play together.* **2** in a group. *The team worked together.*

too /tü/ **1** also. *I am going and Dan is too.* **2** very. *It is too hot.*

took /tu̇k/ past of *take*. See *I took my dog home.*

tooth /tüth/ one of the hard, white parts of the mouth, used for chewing. **teeth.**

tow /tō/ to pull; pull along. *The tugboat had to tow the boat to shore.* **tows, towed, towing.**

town /toun/ a group of houses and buildings, smaller than a city. **towns.**

track /trak/   **1** a line of rails on which a car or train runs. *We walked beside the railroad track.* **2** the mark or footprint of that which has passed. *We saw a track made by a deer.* **tracks.**

trade /trād/ to exchange. *Will you trade your ball for my car?* **trades, traded, trading.**

trail /trāl/   **1** a path for hiking. *Please be sure to follow that trail to the river.* **trails.** **2** to go or be behind. *I always trail behind my mother when we hike.* **trails, trailed, trailing.**

train /trān/   **1** a group of cars, pulled by an engine, that go along a track. **trains.** **2** teach; make fit. *A runner needs to train before a race.* **trains, trained, training.**

tramp /tramp/   **1** a person without a home. **tramps.** **2** walk heavily. *Don't tramp on the floor when the baby's* *sleeping.* **tramps, tramped, tramping.**

treat /trēt/   **1** a gift of something special. *My Mom sometimes has a treat for me when she gets home from work.* **treats.** **2** to act toward, to think of. *I treat my kitten kindly.* **treats, treated, treating.**

tree /trē/ a large plant with a trunk, branches, and leaves. **trees.**

trick /trik/   **1** something done to fool others. *No one can figure out how I did the card trick.* **tricks.** **2** to fool another. *I like to trick my sister by hiding behind the door.* **tricks, tricked, tricking.**

trim /trim/ to make neat or even. *We need to trim the bushes.* **trims, trimmed, trimming.**

trip /trip/   **1** a journey; going somewhere. *We took a trip to the city.* **trips.** **2** to fall. *Don't trip on the broken steps.* **trips, tripped, tripping.**

a	hat
ā	age
ä	far
e	let
ē	equal
ėr	term
i	it
ī	ice
o	hot
ō	open
ô	order
oi	oil
ou	out
u	cup
ù	put
ü	rule
ch	child
ng	long
sh	she
th	thin
ŦH	then
zh	measure

ə = { a in about / e in taken / i in pencil / o in lemon / u in circus

tree

truck /truk/ **1** a large, strong, wheeled object used for carrying things. **trucks.**

try /trī/ to make an effort to do something. *I will try to get it done in time.* **tries, tried, trying.**

tube /tūb/ or /tyüb/ a long pipe that holds something or through which something travels. *This tube of toothpaste is almost empty.* **tubes.**

tug /tug/ **1** a boat that pulls ships; a tugboat. **tugs.** **2** to pull hard. *Don't let the dog tug the rope away!* **tugs, tugged, tugging.**

tune /tün/ or /tyün/ music which is sung or played. *Can you play that tune again?* **tunes.**

twin /twin/ one of two children or animals born from the same mother at the same time. *Twins often look alike.* **twins.**

two /tü/ the number that is one more than one; 2. **twos.**

truck

twin

U

un cle /ung′kəl/ **1** your father's or mother's brother. **2** your aunt's husband. **uncles.**

us /us/ the person speaking plus the person or persons being spoken about. *Please give the paper to us.*

V

ver y /ver′ē/ much; greatly. *We are very happy with our new car.*

W

week end /wēk′end′/ Saturday and Sunday; usually a time when people do not have to work or go to school. **weekends.**

went /went/ past of *go*. See *go. Yesterday he went to the movies.*

were /wėr/ past of *be*. See *be. We were happy.*

west /west/ direction opposite east; where the sun sets. *The early settlers moved west.*

whale /hwāl/ a large animal which lives in the sea. **whales.**

what /hwot/ a word used in asking a question. The thing that. *What happened after school?*

wheel /hwēl/ **1** a round object which turns. *A car cannot go without a wheel.* **wheels.** **2** to turn. *She wheeled the horse away from the tree.* **wheels, wheeled, wheeling.**

where /hwer/ or /hwar/ which or what place. *Where are you going on Sunday?*

while /hwīl/ during or in the time that. *While we were waiting for the doctor, I read three books.*

whirl /hwėrl/ to turn or spin around quickly. *We watched the dancer whirl.* **whirls, whirled, whirling.**

whisk er /hwis′kər/ a hair growing on a man's face or near the mouth of a cat or other animal. *The dog got his whisker wet.* **whiskers.**

whis per /hwis′pər/ **1** to speak low or softly. *Whisper so no one can hear.* **whispers, whispered, whispering.** **2** a low soft sound. *Do you hear the whisper of the wind?* **whispers.**

who /hü/ **1** a word used to ask a question about people. *Who is that leaving in the car?* **2** the person that; any person. *A person who can run fast was asked to be on our team.*

why /hwī/ **1** the reason for. *Why do you ask?* **2** because of. *That is why we are late.*

wide /wīd/ **1** not thin or narrow. *The river is wide.* **2** having a certain distance across. *Our room is ten feet wide.* **wider, widest.**

a	hat
ā	age
ä	far
e	let
ē	equal
ėr	term
i	it
ī	ice
o	hot
ō	open
ô	order
oi	oil
ou	out
u	cup
u̇	put
ü	rule
ch	child
ng	long
sh	she
th	thin
ᵮH	then
zh	measure

ə = ⎧ a in about
　　⎨ e in taken
　　⎪ i in pencil
　　⎪ o in lemon
　　⎩ u in circus

whiskers

wind¹ /wind/ moving air. *The wind blew my hat off my head.* **winds.**

wind² /wīnd/ **1** to roll into a ball. *I will wind this wool into a ball.* **2** to turn in one way and another. *The road winds around the mountain.* **winds, wound, winding.**

wing /wing/ the part of a bird or insect that moves to help it fly. **wings.**

wing

wish /wish/ **1** to want to. *Do you wish to have some help?* **wishes, wished, wishing.** **2** something wanted or hoped for. *Make a wish and it may come true.* **wishes.**

with /wiTH/ or /with/ **1** together in some way. *I always like milk with my lunch.* **2** having. *She is a person with good manners.*

wool /wül/ **1** the fur of a sheep or other animal. **2** material made of wool. *I have a wool hat.*

zebra

XY

yard¹ /yärd/ the ground around a house, school, or other building. *Make sure you stay in the yard.* **yards.**

yard² /yärd/ a unit of measure which is the same as three feet. *The door was one yard wide.* **yards.**

yet /yet/ **1** up until this time. *She has not yet come for a visit.* **2** at this time. *Do you think he is ready yet?*

your /yür/ or /yər/ belonging or having to do with you. *Are these your pencils?*

Z

zebra /ze′brə/ a wild animal that looks something like a horse, but has stripes. *We saw a zebra at the game farm.* **zebras.**

zip /zip/ to close with a

zipper. *Help me zip up my coat.* **zips, zipped, zipping.**

zoo /zü/ a place where animals are kept for people to see. *It is fun to see monkeys at the zoo.* **zoos.**

zoom /züm/ **1** to move upward suddenly. *The wind made the kite zoom above the treetop.* **2** to move very fast. *Watch the car zoom past the house.* **zooms, zoomed, zooming.**

a	hat
ā	age
ä	far
e	let
ē	equal
ėr	term
i	it
ī	ice
o	hot
ō	open
ô	order
oi	oil
ou	out
u	cup
u̇	put
ü	rule
ch	child
ng	long
sh	she
th	thin
ᵺH	then
zh	measure

ə = { a in about
e in taken
i in pencil
o in lemon
u in circus

ZOO

199

UNIT 1

1.

2.

3.

4.

5.

6.

7.

8.

9.

10.

UNIT 2

1.

2.

3.

4.

5.

6.

7.

8.

9.

10.

UNIT 3

1.

2.

3.

4.

5.

6.

7.

8.

9.

10.

POST TESTS

UNIT 4

1. _____
2. _____
3. _____
4. _____
5. _____
6. _____
7. _____
8. _____
9. _____
10. _____

UNIT 5

1. _____
2. _____
3. _____
4. _____
5. _____
6. _____
7. _____
8. _____
9. _____
10. _____

UNIT 7

1. _____
2. _____
3. _____
4. _____
5. _____
6. _____
7. _____
8. _____
9. _____
10. _____

POST TESTS

UNIT 8

1.

2.

3.

4.

5.

6.

7.

8.

9.

10.

UNIT 9

1.

2.

3.

4.

5.

6.

7.

8.

9.

10.

UNIT 10

1.

2.

3.

4.

5.

6.

7.

8.

9.

10.

UNIT 11

1.

2.

3.

4.

5.

6.

7.

8.

9.

10.

UNIT 13

1.

2.

3.

4.

5.

6.

7.

8.

9.

10.

UNIT 14

1.

2.

3.

4.

5.

6.

7.

8.

9.

10.

POST TESTS

UNIT 15

1.

2.

3.

4.

5.

6.

7.

8.

9.

10.

UNIT 16

1.

2.

3.

4.

5.

6.

7.

8.

9.

10.

UNIT 17

1.

2.

3.

4.

5.

6.

7.

8.

9.

10.

UNIT 19

1. _____

2. _____

3. _____

4. _____

5. _____

6. _____

7. _____

8. _____

9. _____

10. _____

UNIT 20

1. _____

2. _____

3. _____

4. _____

5. _____

6. _____

7. _____

8. _____

9. _____

10. _____

UNIT 21

1. _____

2. _____

3. _____

4. _____

5. _____

6. _____

7. _____

8. _____

9. _____

10. _____

POST TESTS

UNIT 22

1. _____
2. _____
3. _____
4. _____
5. _____
6. _____
7. _____
8. _____
9. _____
10. _____

UNIT 23

1. _____
2. _____
3. _____
4. _____
5. _____
6. _____
7. _____
8. _____
9. _____
10. _____

UNIT 25

1. _____
2. _____
3. _____
4. _____
5. _____
6. _____
7. _____
8. _____
9. _____
10. _____

UNIT 26

1.

2.

3.

4.

5.

6.

7.

8.

9.

10.

UNIT 27

1.

2.

3.

4.

5.

6.

7.

8.

9.

10.

UNIT 28

1.

2.

3.

4.

5.

6.

7.

8.

9.

10.

UNIT 29

1.

2.

3.

4.

5.

6.

7.

8.

9.

10.

UNIT 31

1.

2.

3.

4.

5.

6.

7.

8.

9.

10.

UNIT 32

1.

2.

3.

4.

5.

6.

7.

8.

9.

10.

UNIT 33

1. _____

2. _____

3. _____

4. _____

5. _____

6. _____

7. _____

8. _____

9. _____

10. _____

UNIT 34

1. _____

2. _____

3. _____

4. _____

5. _____

6. _____

7. _____

8. _____

9. _____

10. _____

UNIT 35

1. _____

2. _____

3. _____

4. _____

5. _____

6. _____

7. _____

8. _____

9. _____

10. _____

UNIT 6

1. _____

2. _____

3. _____

4. _____

5. _____

6. _____

7. _____

8. _____

9. _____

10. _____

11. _____

12. _____

13. _____

14. _____

15. _____

16. _____

17. _____

18. _____

19. _____

20. _____

21. _____

22. _____

23. _____

24. _____

25. _____

UNIT 12

1. _____

2. _____

3. _____

4. _____

5. _____

6. _____

7. _____

8. _____

9. _____

10. _____

11. _____

12. _____

13. _____

14. _____

15. _____

16. _____

17. _____

18. _____

19. _____

20. _____

21. _____

22. _____

23. _____

24. _____

25. _____

UNIT 18

1. _____

2. _____

3. _____

4. _____

5. _____

6. _____

7. _____

8. _____

9. _____

10. _____

11. _____

12. _____

13. _____

14. _____

15. _____

16. _____

17. _____

18. _____

19. _____

20. _____

21. _____

22. _____

23. _____

24. _____

25. _____

UNIT 24

1. _____

2. _____

3. _____

4. _____

5. _____

6. _____

7. _____

8. _____

9. _____

10. _____

11. _____

12. _____

13. _____

14. _____

15. _____

16. _____

17. _____

18. _____

19. _____

20. _____

21. _____

22. _____

23. _____

24. _____

25. _____

UNIT 30

1.

2.

3.

4.

5.

6.

7.

8.

9.

10.

11.

12.

13.

14.

15.

16.

17.

18.

19.

20.

21.

22.

23.

24.

25.

UNIT 36

1. _____

2. _____

3. _____

4. _____

5. _____

6. _____

7. _____

8. _____

9. _____

10. _____

11. _____

12. _____

13. _____

14. _____

15. _____

16. _____

17. _____

18. _____

19. _____

20. _____

21. _____

22. _____

23. _____

24. _____

25. _____

CREDITS

PHOTOGRAPHS

ILLUSTRATIONS